FAIL BETTER!

FAIL BETTER!

STUMBLING TO SUCCESS IN
SALES & MARKETING

 25 REMARKABLE RENEGADES SHOW HOW

STEPHEN BROWN

CYAN

Marshall Cavendish
Business

Copyright © 2008 Stephen Brown

First published in 2008 by:

Marshall Cavendish Limited
Fifth Floor
32–38 Saffron Hill
London EC1N 8FH
United Kingdom
T: +44 (0)20 7421 8120
F: +44 (0)20 7421 8121
sales@marshallcavendish.co.uk
www.marshallcavendish.co.uk

and

Cyan Communications Limited
5th Floor (Marshall Cavendish)
32–38 Saffron Hill
London EC1N 8FH
United Kingdom
T: +44 (0)20 7421 8145
F: +44 (0)20 7421 8146
sales@cyanbooks.com
www.cyanbooks.com

A CIP record for this book is available from the British Library

ISBN-13: 978-0-462-09904-0
ISBN-10: 0-462-09904-0

Printed and bound in Great Britain by
Mackays of Chatham Limited, Chatham, Kent

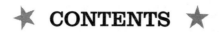

★ CONTENTS ★

★ AN INTRODUCTORY KICK ★ IN THE TEETH

Who is the greatest marketer in the world today? Steve Jobs? Donald Trump? Madonna? Michael O'Leary? It is difficult if not impossible to choose, though the very fact that Jobs, Trump, Madonna, and O'Leary need no introduction says a lot about their top-drawer marketing abilities. We all know who they are. We'd all like to possess their remarkable marketing prowess.

The really remarkable thing about Jobs and co., I believe, is that their marketing practices run counter to conventional wisdom. Far from being customer obsessed, as traditional textbooks recommend, they are customer opposed. Opposed to the point of offensiveness. Michael O'Leary tells refund-seeking customers to fuck off. Madonna invites encore-demanding audiences to swivel on it. Donald Trump boasts of his ability to hoodwink customers with "truthful hyperbole." Steve Jobs makes life difficult for die-hard Apple fans and brings brilliantly successful products to market without an iota of consumer research.

O'Leary *et al.* are successful failures. According to received marketing wisdom, they should have failed ignominiously. Yet they're the best in the business. They sinned to win. They are commercial nonconformists. They succeeded *despite* established marketing principles, not *because* of them.

The Trump company, of course, aren't paragons of unprincipled virtue. Without exception, they have had their ups and downs. Casino-owner Donald Trump diced with bankruptcy on several occasions. Many thought Madonna was history after her obscene rant on *Letterman*. Michael O'Leary's ambitious plans for Ryanair, not least his shock-horror attempts to acquire Aer Lingus, have been repeatedly thwarted by the Irish government. For every iPod-ish triumph, Steve Jobs has suffered a Lisa-like defeat. The recently released iPhone, for all we know, may go the way of the Newton rather than the Mac.

Failure, however, comes with the territory. History shows that the highest achievers in business life consistently fail their way to the top. They know what it's like to stare down the barrel of defeat:

★ Colonel Harland Saunders, the marketing genius behind KFC, failed at just about every job imaginable – soldier, lawyer, train driver, ferryboat operator, mule wrangler, tyre salesman, petrol station impresario – before he hit upon a method of franchising fried chicken in the 1950s. He was 62 at the time.

★ Joe Girard, listed in the *Guinness Book of Records* as the most successful car salesman ever, struggled for years in the construction industry. He somehow managed to do the impossible by going bust during America's post-war housing boom. Hampered by a serious speech impediment, he went into automobile sales as a last resort. He persuaded a local car dealer to take him on, cold-called prospects day after day without reward, and eventually got lucky late one evening when he was the only salesperson on duty. Stuttering Joe never looked back.

★ Ruth Handler, the brains behind Barbie, faced fierce opposition within Mattel when she suggested that there was a demand for grown-up dolls. The design team baulked, executives quit in disgust, pre-launch market research was uniformly negative, and toyshops refused to carry the busty creation. But within three months, Mattel was selling 20,000 Barbies a week and, Bratz notwithstanding, the 48-year-old doll is still going strong.

Would that everyone's endeavours ended as happily as Handler's, but failure is the norm in business life. Eight out of ten Hollywood movies fail, one breaks even, and one's a box-office blockbuster. Similar ratios are reported in the publishing industry, in the music business, in the restaurant racket, in the bowels of big pharma, and in companies like toiletries titan Johnson & Johnson, which claims that "failure is our most important product." Felix Dennis, the multi-millionaire media mogul, goes even further when he says: "After a lifetime of making money and observing better men and women than I fall by the wayside, I am convinced that fear of failing in the eyes of the world is the single biggest impediment to amassing wealth."[1]

So fearsome is the fear of failure that most marketing gurus pretend it doesn't exist. They are reluctant to mention the F-word. The vast majority of their how-to books focus on success, on triumph, on winning business, on happy-ever-after fairy stories. Now, this is all fine and dandy. It acts as a kind of corporate comfort-blanket. But if we really want to make sense of, say, why Oprah Winfrey is the staggering success she is today, it's useful to know that she was sacked from her first job as a newsreader and unceremoniously informed, "You're not fit for TV."

If we wish to get a handle on Sir Philip Green, Great Britain's pre-eminent retailer and the country's seventh wealthiest man, it is important to appreciate that he failed to shine at school, that his first fifteen years in the rag trade were marked by a series of calamitous failures, not least a line of Joan Collins designer jeans, and that his failure to acquire Marks & Spencer (on two occasions) probably did more to establish his stellar retailing reputation than his achievements at Bhs and Arcadia.

If we want to know how Miuccia put the devil in Prada, it's worth noting that almost every step of her illustrious career was a classic case of "failing up." A communist, feminist, doctorate-holding mime artist, she joined the family leatherwear firm with considerable reluctance; had to have her arm twisted to diversify into apparel and expand the Prada brand; and to this very day refuses to play safe with her collections, preferring to run the risk of catastrophic failure than pander to consumer expectations or operate within the fashion comfort zone.

If we wonder, as every supermarket shopper surely does, where the Birds Eye brand of frozen foods comes from, we find ourselves in a heart-warming tale of if-at-first-you-don't-succeed. On a visit to the Arctic wastes in 1912, Clarence Birdseye was deeply impressed by the Inuits' ability to keep fish fresh by flash freezing. He was convinced that he'd discovered the Northwest Passage of domestic comestibles. So convinced, in fact, that failure after failure after failure to find a market didn't put off the Frobisher of frozen foodstuffs. He finally broke through the pack ice of consumer resistance in 1930 and Birds Eye has been with us ever since.[2]

If, in short, we want to better understand business in general and marketing in particular, we need to focus on failures: on those who stumbled their way to success, sinned to win, challenged orthodoxy, overcame adversity, and learned from their marketing mistakes. As serial failure Walt Disney once astutely observed, "You may not realize it when it happens, but a kick in the teeth may be the best thing in the world for you."

That's what this book is about: those who are forged by failure, steeled to succeed. It argues that there are six essential A-ttributes shared by fail better over-achievers: *Ambition, Activity, Astigmatism, Amplification, Aphorism* and *Ambiguity*. However, let's not get ahead of ourselves ...

★ 1 ★

THE FAILGOOD FACTOR

Fifty years ago, the US premiere of *Waiting for Godot* opened at the Coconut Grove Playhouse, Miami. Starring Tom Ewell and Bert Lahr, it was ambitiously billed as "the laugh sensation of two continents." Now, theatrical productions are a law unto themselves, as everyone knows, but the Coconut Grove billing must rank among the greatest overstatements in the history of the boards. Beckett's nihilistic play was neither a comedy (though it contained comedic elements) nor the laugh sensation of a single continent, let alone two. Rather it was a play where, as one early commentator memorably observed, "nothing happens, twice."

Nothing happened at the Miami box office either. *Godot* was a disaster and went dark after two weeks. It almost closed in London, too, after the first performances were greeted with derision, catcalls and wholesale audience walkouts. Nowadays universally acclaimed, Sam Beckett's masterpiece nearly didn't make its Parisian debut at all and got mounted only thanks to a tiny government grant for foreign playwrights writing in French. The extremely low staging costs – four actors, one boy, and a spartan set – also helped swing things in its favour, as did the scandalized reaction of early reviewers (which always draws a crowd).

Had *Godot* failed, it would have been entirely in keeping

with Beckett's career trajectory up to that point. His first novel, for example, was rejected on no fewer than 42 occasions before finally finding a publisher in 1938. Understandably, the Nobel Prize winner later penned the plangent words that every former failure lives by: "Ever tried. Ever failed. No matter. Try again. Fail again. Fail better."[1]

Failure may not be fun, especially for those at the receiving end, but it's fascinating all the same. As a leading failure adviser – yes, such people do exist – recalls about his years on the calamity circuit, "I've taught tens of thousands of business executives in my seminars and even more university students than that over the years. Whenever I talk about failures, mistakes, errors, whatever you want to call them, I can see my audience's interest level rise dramatically ... I've found out, too, that they remembered the concepts I talked about in conjunction with the failures more than they remembered the concepts I talked about in conjunction with the success stories I gave them."[2]

It's hard to disagree. Whatever else he did in his long career, Decca's Dick Rowe will always be remembered for failing to sign The Beatles. Whatever else he did during his long career, the Grand Ole Opry's Jim Denny will be remembered as the man who told a young Elvis Presley "You ain't going nowhere, son, you ought to go back to drivin' a truck." Whatever else he achieved in his career as the *New York Post*'s movie reviewer, Jim Simon will be remembered as the man who considered *Star Wars* "as exciting as last year's weather reports." Whatever else he achieves in his glittering career, literary agent Barry Cunningham will always be remembered as the man who informed J. K. Rowling "You'll never make any money out of children's books, Jo."

Failure is the New Success

Unforgettable failures aren't confined to the cultural industries, furthermore. Only a churl could fail to take pleasure in former vice-president Dan Quayle's failure to spell "potatoe" correctly during an infamous high-school visit. Chastened and contrite, he later added "I should have caught the mistake, but as Mark Twain once said, 'You should never trust a man who has only one way to spell a word.'" Except that the quote came from President Andrew Jackson. Chastened and contrite, Quayle later added "I should have remembered it was Andrew Jackson who said that, since he got his nickname 'Stonewall' by vetoing bills passed by Congress." Except that President Andrew Jackson wasn't called "Stonewall." That was another Jackson entirely, the celebrated Confederate general Thomas J. Jackson. Desperate Dan would have done well to spell out the old saying, "When your inn a whole, stopp diggine."

Dan Quayle, to be sure, is no Jack Kennedy, let alone an Abe Lincoln. Yet even the very highest achievers stumble repeatedly on the rocky road to success:

★ Abe Lincoln failed to get elected to Congress on three occasions, tried and failed to secure a seat in the Senate, then ran for the vice-presidency unsuccessfully before becoming the fourteenth president of the United States.

★ Albert Einstein was a dunce at school, dismissed by his teachers as a no-hoper who couldn't do sums to save his life. He looked set for a career of quiet desperation in the Swiss patent office. Then he had a brainwave about relativity and changed our understanding of the universe.

★ Thomas Edison, the inventor's inventor, famously failed 6,000 times while testing filaments for the first commercially viable electric light bulb. Little wonder he subsequently concluded that success is 1 part inspiration to 99 parts perspiration.

★ Isadora Duncan was the laughing-stock of the professional
dance community, an untutored amateur who couldn't do
a *pas de deux*, much less pose *en pointe*. But her free-
flowing, Delsarte-inspired movements tore up the terpsi-
chorean prairie and inspired what we now know as modern
dance.

★ Michael Jordan, possibly the pre-eminent professional
athlete of the late twentieth century, was cut from the
roster of his college basketball team because his coach
couldn't detect a scintilla of ability. Boy, did he prove that
coach wrong.

★ Nelson Mandela was a terrorist who advocated the use of
extreme violence, practised what he preached, and paid
the price with a prison sentence. He came to his senses,
commenced the long walk to reconciliation, and joined the
noble pantheon of Nobel Peace Prize winners.

★ David Attenborough, the much-admired British naturalist
whose landmark wildlife programmes remain the bench-
mark for television documentaries, failed his BBC screen-
test in 1952. His speaking voice, that wonderful
Attenborough burr, was considered perfectly acceptable,
but his teeth were too, well, fang-like for the British
viewing public, even the wildlife lovers among them.[3]

There's No Business Like No Business

Failure looms large in every walk of life, but it looms largest of
all in business. Although management gurus constantly chant
the mantra of success – how to attain it, how to sustain it, how
to unearth it, how to unleash it – the sad reality is that the vast
majority of business ventures fail. Most companies collapse,
most start-ups stop, most mergers misfire, most innovations
implode, most CEOs crater, most R&D founders, most long-

range forecasts flub and most business "success stories" have a back story full of blunders, clangers, *faux pas*, errors of judgement, call them what you will.[4]

Henry Ford, for example, was a complete flop for much of his early career. He abandoned the family farm, toiled unsuccessfully for Thomas Edison, developed an electric car during his spare time, and earned the nickname Crazy Henry for his trouble. In 1899, he formed the Detroit Automobile Company, which quickly hit the skids without producing any products. Undeterred, he founded the Ford Motor Company in 1903 and made a series of high-price, low-volume, top-of-the-market autos with strictly limited success. After a Damascene conversion to the cause of cut-price/high-volume production, Henry came up with the radical Model N. It promptly bit the dust. Ford went back to the drawing board and finally hit pay-dirt in 1908 with the celebrated Model T.

Walt Disney hadn't a friend in the world. And no wonder. When he wasn't irritable, he was irascible. With intolerance on top. Ornery doesn't begin to describe him. He wouldn't listen to reason. He couldn't hear what everyone in the movie business was telling him. Namely, that his experimental short film *Steamboat Willie*, featuring a ferret-faced mouse with a squeaky voice, was certain to flatline at the box office. But it was Walt's last fling. He'd failed in his attempt to become a newspaper cartoonist in Kansas City. He'd moved to Hollywood and, after the usual Tinseltown disappointments, finally broke through with *Oswald the Lucky Rabbit*, only to discover that his distributor owned the rights to everything, Oswald's lucky paws included. He'd been royally ripped off and his employees had defected to boot. So, in desperation, the man became a mouse. Walt's first two Mickey Mouse adventures, *Plane Crazy* and *The Gallopin' Gaucho*, failed to make an impact. He went for broke with the third, despite the sceptics. The naysayers were wrong. The world went wild for *Steamboat Willie*. The rest is Disney history.

Elsa Schiaparelli may have been the doyenne of haute couture during the Great Depression, she may have been Coco Chanel's principal competitor, she may have been a pioneer of new technologies such as rayon, zip fasteners and animal-skin prints, and she may have been responsible for many of the developments that today's fashionistas take for granted, especially those who subscribe to the Vivienne Westwood/Zandra Rhodes school of shocking frocks. But Schiaparelli didn't start out that way. On the contrary, she struggled manfully against insuperable odds. She came from a conservative Italian family. She failed as a surrealist poet, married a penniless evangelist, spread the good word door to door, followed her calling to the United States, and earned a crust in various dead-end jobs – freelance translator, Wall Street gofer, silent movie stand-in – before finding herself in the Parisian fashion business, where her first couture house, Maison Lambal, cratered in less than a year. Yet she still went on to greatness.

Earl Tupper was a dreamer. He dreamed of a perfect world encased in plastic. Instead of tending to his tree-surgery business, he read self-help books, did correspondence courses in marketing, and came up with all manner of get-rich-quick schemes. He dabbled unsuccessfully in plastic toys, plastic ducks, plastic belts, plastic jewellery, plastic dishracks, plastic cigarette holders, plastic knitting needles, plastic garter hooks and, although plastic cards escaped him, he even hatched a plan for plastic corsets. Sadly, his fantastic plastic underwear was ahead of its time. Plastic containers, however, were something else again. Earl's range of kitchen containers caused a sensation in the early 1950s. Tupperware received all sorts of design awards, *Good Housekeeping* commendations, and dramatic displays in high-class department stores. It didn't sell, unfortunately. Until a marketing genius intervened. Brownie Wise, an ambitious single mother, came up with the party-plan method of moving the merchandise and, with the enthusiastic support of a predominantly female salesforce, Brownie turned

Tupper's going-nowhere-fast invention into a must-have marketing triumph.

Sir James Dyson is Earl Tupper's direct descendant. Granted, Dyson is a public-school-educated Englishman, as opposed to a self-taught, self-made, self-stacking New Englander. Nevertheless, the parallels are there for all to see. For plastic corsets, read wheelbarrows with a ball. For plastic cigarette holders, read New Age hand-driers for public conveniences. For plastic dishracks, read a rinky-dink launch mechanism for amphibious automobiles, the so-called Trolleyball. For Tupper's propensity to proselytize about plastic, read Dyson's rants on innovation, design, and Britain's diminishing manufacturing base (an argument undermined by Dyson's own decision to defect to Malaysia). For Earl's eponymous Tupperware, read Sir James's cyclonic vacuum cleaner, the invention that took a dozen years and 5,172 prototypes to develop. A development, moreover, that took place in the face of relentless ridicule, repeated rejection, and restricted resources. But Dyson never said die. No siree. His bagless wonder broke the mould, reinvented the vacuum-cleaner business, and not only ground his competitors into the dirt but hoovered them up for good measure.

If At First

Failure sucks, no doubt about it. Yet Dyson, Ford, Disney, Schiaparelli, and so forth demonstrate that failure needn't be fatal. They also show that success isn't unattainable. Determination, perseverance, endeavour, and sheer bloody-mindedness can pay prodigious dividends. Hanging in there despite repeated failure, abject failure, heart-wrenching failure is what separates the hotshots from the have-nots in many walks of life, though success isn't guaranteed. Just ask Jane Austen, Vincent van Gogh, Emily Dickinson, Herman Melville, Gregor Mendel or Friedrich Nietzsche, all of whom laboured heroically for scant recognition throughout their sadly unfulfilled lifetimes.

Indeed, even when success is tenaciously attained, it is infuriatingly fickle, fleeting, fragile, fitful, as most of the foregoing figures found out. Honest Abe Lincoln was assassinated at the age of 56. Albert Einstein couldn't accept quantum theory and struggled unsuccessfully to refute it. Thomas Edison's astounding electrical triumphs – phonograph, stock ticker, movie camera, etc. – must be set against his resounding defeat in the current wars, when his DC system was trumped by Tesla's AC. Isadora Duncan descended into an embarrassing parody of her former self before she took her final scarf-wrapped bow under the wheels of a speeding sports car. Ford's Model T was overtaken by Sloan's General Motors range in the late 1920s and, as for the Edsel, only the *Titanic* ranks higher in the pantheon of new product failures. Earl Tupper quarrelled with Brownie Wise, the person who turned his plastic daydream into dollar-spinning reality, and the iconic magic of Tupperware rapidly evaporated.[5]

Walt Disney, in fairness, fared better than most because he bet the farm successfully on several post-*Steamboat Willie* occasions – *Snow White*, Disneyland, the 1950s TV series – despite a chorus of Cassandras. But even Walt came a cropper with *Fantasia*, ruined his avuncular reputation with a series of brutal strike-breaking steps, and eventually left a legacy of saccharine, family-focused productions that constrained his studio for decades and almost brought about its demise in the 1980s. The less said about Euro Disney and latter-day boardroom shenanigans, the better.

The Tripping Point

Tough to attain, success is even tougher to sustain. Failure is always lurking, looming, loitering with intent. Airbus, for instance, went *mano a mano* with Boeing, the Battler from

Seattle, and succeeded brilliantly thanks to a suite of comfortable, economical, state-of-the-art airliners. Emboldened, Airbus gambled its future on a superjumbo, the A380, and failed to deliver on schedule. Customers are reconsidering their options and the back-on-top Battler can't believe its luck.

Sony, similarly, has recently gone walkabout. Being beaten to the iPod punch is one thing, failure to ship the PlayStation 3 on schedule is another. Getting caught up in a DVD format standoff is something else again. Shades of Betamax. But installing combustible batteries in the pricey Vaio laptop is suggestive of serious smarts-fatigue.

Having coped admirably with the New Coke debacle of the mid-1980s, Coca-Cola is on the ropes once more. Contamination scares in Belgium and India, a disastrous foray into bottled water in Britain, and the rise of anti-Americanism in the aftermath of Iraq have inflicted untold damage on the world's biggest brand.

Lego, likewise, has lost its way in the pre-teen market maze. After 70 years of sustained success, worldwide popularity, and brand recognition to die for, the conservative toy company went wild and crazy with a diversification programme that included apparel, watches, video games, and the lucre-led lure of lifestyle marketing. There's no fool like an old fool. Factories are closing, long-term employees are getting axed, theme parks are being sold off as a job lot, and the firm's future prosperity is increasingly linked to movie tie-ins. Now there's a dependable partner.

Time has been called too on Carphone Warehouse's incredible ascent. From its lowly 1980s origins in an East London lock-up, the one-stop shop for mobile phone paraphernalia successfully surfed successive waves of telecommunications innovation, turning CEO Charles Dunstone into a celebrity suit along the way. However, a perfect storm of defecting suppliers, unwise acquisitions, and a disastrous sales promotion for free broadband hit the Warehouse unawares in autumn 2006. Who knows which way the business wind blows?

Even Wal-Mart's march to TOTAL GLOBAL DOMINATION – cue maniacal laughter and stroking of malevolent pussycat – has been halted in its tracks by the honest burghers of Germany. The Beast from Bentonville invaded in 1997, all guns blazing, and it expected Deutschland to surrender without demur. The indigenous retailers are a hardy breed, however. Aldi, Lidl, *et al.* have been fighting guerrilla price wars since they were knee-high to 7-Eleven, and German citizens are understandably chary of dictatorial companies with retail *Lebensraum* in mind. Roundly defeated, the Beast beat a retreat in 2006. It remains to be seen whether Germany is Wal-Mart's Stalingrad, but consumer resistance to its draconian regime is mounting worldwide. The thousand-year retailer is rattled. Tesco, the plucky grocery chain from Blighty, is set to invade Wal-Mart's American heartland. Inspired by the German insurgents, it is confident of success Stateside. Every Lidl helps.

Come Back to the Five and Dime, Ronald McDonald

Wal-Mart may well recover from its stumble, as may Lego, Coke, Sony, Airbus, and the others. Business life is a rickety roller-coaster. Only a few years ago, McDonald's was suffering from arteriosclerosis, Marks & Spencer was out of fashion, Kate Moss's modelling career was snowed under, Burberry was beset by the deadly chav virus, Penguin Books had its logistics in a twist, Ikea-rage was rampant among disgruntled customers, Nike was trampling over Third World workers rather than walking on Air Max, Nokia needed to call a friend but couldn't get through on its clunky cellphones, and mighty, mighty Microsoft was being rattled by Linux, legal proceedings, and Apple's remarkable resurgence. All have recovered their equipoise. Temporarily, at least.

Others have failed so comprehensively that full recovery is inconceivable. The not-so-good ship Parmalat is drifting in a sea of rancid yogurt. Enron, Tyco, WorldCom, and the rest of the millennial malefactors have fallen into the pit of eternal damnation. The Michael Jackson brand is so badly tainted that his once admirable marketing abilities have been forgotten by all but the most ardent devotees. Tom Cruise may find it difficult to recover from the shock of Sumner Redstone's summary dismissal, though if anyone can grin his way out of trouble, it's the Sunny Delight of showbusiness.

Sunny Delight, in case you've forgotten, is a feisty fruit drink that took off like a rocket but plummeted to earth when parents discovered that it contained more chemicals than Pete Doherty's medicine cabinet. Sunny D, nevertheless, epitomizes the zero-to-hero-to-zero trajectory of western capitalism, though it'll never warrant inclusion in the failure hall of fame. The latter includes such titans as the board-game executive at Parker Brothers who turned down Monopoly; the anonymous employee at Kodak who spurned Polaroid's instant-photography technology; the bright spark at IBM who wasn't interested in the plain-paper copier developed by Chester "Xerox" Carlson; the director of *Gone With the Wind*, Victor Fleming, who opted for a flat fee rather than 20 percent of the profits because he thought the film would be the "biggest white elephant of all time"; the irrepressible jewellery retailer Gerald Ratner, who called his company's products "total crap" and has rued the day ever since; the chairman of Barclays Bank, Matthew Barrett, who 'fessed up to the fact that Barclaycards are a right royal rip-off; and – get this, customer huggers – Topshop's David Shepherd, who described his target market as "hooligans or whatever," then added insult to injury with "Very few of our customers have to wear suits to work ... they'll be for his first interview or court case."[6]

What Goes Up

However, before you mock the clairvoyantly challenged or point the finger at foot-in-mouth-afflicted executives, it's necessary to note that success and failure are two sides of the same coin. Like Kipling's twin impostors of triumph and disaster, they are not only closely related, but inseparably conjoined. The one begets the other. Just as failure is the breeding-ground of success, so success is the Fallopian tube of failure. As many commentators have noted, success is often accompanied by complacency, conceit, and a cocksure conviction that collapse cannot happen. Success can also give rise to conservatism, the mistaken belief that what worked well in the past will continue to work well in the future. Caution replaces creativity, rigid thinking supplants risk taking, buccaneering innovation becomes bureaucratic inertia.

IBM, for instance, imploded cataclysmically in 1992, a consequence of the company's continued dependence on the declining mainframe market, coupled with its bureaucratic inability to leverage its early-1980s lead in the PC sector. Its wretched PCjr, an under-powered, over-priced, modem-less laptop, and a troublesome operating system called Top View – nicknamed Top Heavy by disgruntled customers – all failed disastrously. Yet such was IBM's arrogance, it haughtily ignored such upstart competitors as Microsoft, Intel, and Oracle until it was far too late. In 1992, Big Blue announced a loss of $5 billion, saw its share price fall from $100 to $48, and shed 43,000 employees who'd erroneously imagined they had jobs for life.

Hollinger, a Canadian property, mining, and publishing conglomerate, burgeoned under the rambunctious leadership of Conrad Black. This culminated in the spectacular capture of the Telegraph Group, a British national institution. Prompted, however, by his staggeringly ambitious significant other – allegedly, Your Honour – Conrad Black descended to the dark side, indulged in a little bit of light-fingered corporate chicanery, and started treating the company as his personal petty-cash box (just the odd private jet, New York mansion, and Louis XIV theme party, m'lud). The Feds were not amused. The penitentiary awaits. How art the Hollinger fallen.

Benetton bedazzled the world with its vibrant apparel, funky boutiques, fast-response replenishment systems, irrepressible Italian pizzazz, and brilliantly successful advertising campaigns. Brainchild of ace photographer Oliver Toscani, the United Colours campaign included provocative images of AIDS victims, car bombs, newborn babies, *in flagrante* nuns, and, most revolting of all, the CEO in his birthday suit. It earned worldwide condemnation, ever-mounting sales and, ultimately, the hubristic belief that Toscani could get away with anything. Nemesis came in the form of a capital punishment photoshoot that featured a convicted murderer on Death Row. Understandably outraged, the murder victim's family protested vigorously, the American media took up their case, and before long the Toscani-led campaign collapsed around Benetton's ears, wrecking its reputation.

P-P-P-Pick Up a Paradox

Benetton's, Black's, and Big Blue's embarrassments are testament to the terrible twins of triumph and disaster. Locked in a mutually dependent dialectic, they are the yin and yang of business, the Tao of commerce. As Farson and Keyes observe in *The Innovation Paradox*: "Nearly any apparent success can lead to failure if care isn't taken … The modern histories of America's one-time most successful companies – IBM, Xerox, Eastman Kodak, Polaroid – read like the same story with interchangeable characters. The plots seldom vary. Like a huge army, a big company wins victories, dominates its market, gets bigger, develops rigid systems, resists change, then nearly succumbs to ragtag guerrilla bands living off the land."[7]

Danny Miller goes even further than this "fat cat" hypothesis. In *The Icarus Paradox*, he shows that the very qualities responsible for sending an organization soaring Icarus-like above the clouds also tempt it too close to the sun and precipitate its hubristic fall from grace.[8] The pre-plummet pattern, Miller maintains, differs from company to company, but the outcome is always the same. Technology-led "craftsmen" like Texas Instruments and DEC evolve into production-obsessed "tinkerers"; merger-minded "builders" such as ITT and Dome Petroleum become swaggering "imperialists," absorbing all and sundry into unmanageable conglomerates; innovation-inclined "pioneers" akin to Apple and Wang lose touch with reality in general and consumers in particular as they morph into otherworldly "utopians"; and marketing-oriented "salesmen" *à la* P&G and A&P lose the plot, become preoccupied with image, style, brand equity, etc., and end up as directionless "drifters." As if.

According to Miller, the four paradigmatic trajectories – "focusing," "venturing," "inventing," and "decoupling," he calls them – are virtually unavoidable. The singular talents that propel a start-up along the high road to success are the same attributes that lead to ruination on the low road of failure. Competences, he contends, can kill if care isn't taken, a clear head isn't kept, conceit isn't contained, and complacency isn't confronted.

Nowhere is the hubris/nemesis dialectic better illustrated than in the lunatic case of Boo.com, the Icarus of the Internet. Inspired by Amazon's business model and intoxicated by the irrational exuberance of the early e-tail era, Swedish founders Ernst Malmsten and Kajsa Leander set out to do a Bezos on brand-name sportswear. Their idea was great, if you subscribe to the mistaken notion of first-mover advantage. Their website was wonderful, if you were one of the few with the broadband capacity to download its Flash-animated features. Their pre-launch, multi-country advertising campaign was unforgettable, if you're inspired by the sight of subscribers vomiting into a bucket. Their initial sales volumes were impressive, if you accept that generating $200,000 in revenue is a good return for Boo's $20 million per month "burn rate." Their company was competently managed, if you believe that $120 million of investors' money should be spent on fancy offices, expensive furnishings, generous freebies for friends in the media, and the adoption of a jetset lifestyle by the founders before a single item of sportswear had been shipped. And that unlimited free returns, in a jumped-up mail-order business, wouldn't be a serious problem ...

Needless to say, less than a year after its rocket-powered launch, Boo.com burned up on re-entry.[9] Actually, it didn't even get into low earth orbit. Malmsten and Leander would've been better off using wax wings and calling the company Icarus.com.

Hey Daedalus, squeeze this.

★ 2 ★

BRING ON THE EMPTY MARKETERS

D avid Niven, the suave English superstar of Hollywood's golden age, tells numerous humorous anecdotes of his heroic failures in Tinseltown. He also tells the tale of émigré director George Cukor, whose command of the English language left a lot to be desired. While working on a complicated battle scene involving riderless chargers, the lapsed-Hungarian director bellowed out in broken English, "Bring on the empty horses."[1]

As Hollywood one-liners go, Cukor's garbled instructions aren't in the same league as Sam Goldwyn's comment on greedy stars who "bite the hand that lays the golden egg," or W. C. Fields' dipsomaniacal dismissal of drinking water, "fish fuck in it," or Mae West's account of her infamous chastity fatigue, "I used to be Snow White, and then I drifted." Nevertheless it is time, my friends, to bring on the empty marketers.

Now, you don't need me to tell you that the customer-oriented marketing concept dates from the mid-1950s. The notion of customer-centricity – focusing the entire organization on the ultimate consumer's needs – was developed by the immortal Peter Drucker, popularized by the late great Ted Levitt, and codified by the peerless Philip Kotler in his bestselling, much-imitated marketing primers. So successfully did Pete, Ted, and Phil promote the idea of customer orientation that very few realize that "marketing" began as a management fad, akin to "excellence," "six sigma," or the "balanced scorecard."[2]

Marketing is not only the most successful management fad of all time, it is touted as a fail-safe method of avoiding failure. Unlike countless fly-by-night management bromides – mentioning no names – the marketing concept really works. If you find out what your customers want and meet their needs better than the competition, then success is sure to follow. The process is simplicity itself, moreover, though its implementation and sustenance are easier said than done.

In practice, of course, marketing's record is patchy at best and appalling at worst. Despite the finest market research that money can buy; despite detailed situation analyses of the likely fit between marketplace opportunities, corporate capabilities, and competitor activities; despite sophisticated marketing plans, strategies, and campaigns, all mounted with military precision; despite the stupendous brainpower of innumerable B-school-based thinkers, teachers, and theoreticians – collective gasp! – the fact of the matter is that marketing's successes are surpassed by its failures. Empirical studies show that most new products fail, and if anything the failure rate is increasing. Empirical studies show that most brand extensions flop, and if anything they undermine the original brand's laboriously established reputation. Empirical studies show that most advertising is ignored, and if anything its in-your-face ubiquity is antagonizing the very people it's supposed to attract. At the same time, we still don't know which half of an advertising campaign works, or the half of the half that cuts through the clutter, or the half of the half of the half that stimulates consumer desire, or the half of the half of the half of the half that results in a purchase (half of which will be returned as unsuitable, unsatisfactory, or otherwise inappropriate).

At the Going Down of the Sales, We Will Remember Them

Marketing, let's be frank, is the Guadalcanal of capitalism, a corporate killing field. Our fallen are legion. Moonshine Aftershave, Oasis Deodorant, Batman Crazy Foam, Gimme Cucumber Hair Conditioner, Buffalo Chip Chocolate Cookies, I Hate Peas, I Hate Beets, I Hate Spinach are just some of the many rookie products that died for their company. The soft drinks category alone is brands' Bataan. Hagar the Horrible Cola, Okeechobee Orange Pokem, Kickapoo Joy Juice, Yabba Dabba Dew, Panda Punch, Sudden Soda.[3] Where are they now?

Where indeed are those who remember Tingle Pants, a Lycra swimwear ensemble with stereo speakers in the crotch? Eat my shorts, iPod! How many of you old-timers played Ultrashock, an arcade game that rewarded winners with a hair-raising electric shock? Don King was a fan, presumably. Who, if anyone, was unwise enough to spend $20 on the Two-Potato Clock, a novelty timepiece that ran off the energy generated when electrodes are placed in a slightly acidic medium such as potatoes? Dan Quayle, possibly. What, furthermore, possessed a manufacturer of personal protection devices to come up with Skunk Guard, a quick-crush capsule that spurted eau de skunk all over the assailant? True, the stink lingered, thereby facilitating easy identification of the miscreant, but buried by handbag clutter, the Skunk Guard capsules were prone to impromptu breakages. Yuck, yuck, and thrice yuck.

The really frightening thing, amigos, is that Skunk Guard, Two-Potato Clock, and Tingle Pants *actually made it to market*. Just think of all the ideas that never arrive. A comprehensive 1980s study by Booz Allen & Hamilton found that only 14 percent of companies' new business ideas are brought to market.[4] That percentage, moreover, doesn't include ideas generated outside companies by garden-shed inventors, self-employed entrepreneurs, and freelance crackpots. You know the kind of people I mean, the quasi-crazies who get singed in the *Dragons' Den*, a semi-reality TV programme that gives gizmo-makers an opportunity to pitch their products to a panel of experts in the hope of attracting financial backing. Tingle Pants is a stroke of genius compared to some of the pitches made by *Dragons' Den* denizens.

Don't ask ... just don't ask.

It's easy to laugh at the DDDs (*Dragons' Den* Discards), though at least they had the bottle to make their pitch.[5] The history of innovation shows that laughter plus disparagement is often people's first reaction to new ideas. As an early adopter of postmodern marketing principles – once wacko, now accepted – I can personally testify to this tee-hee tendency. I'm accordingly inclined to concur with eminent British biologist J. B. S. Haldane, who claimed that there are four stages of idea acceptance: (1) this is worthless nonsense; (2) this is an interesting but perverse point of view; (3) this is true but quite unimportant; (4) I always said so.[6]

The point I'm making is that even the most carefully formulated, richly resourced, and painstakingly implemented marketing endeavours can, like Robbie Burns' best-laid schemes o' mice an' men, gang aft a-gley. As everyone knows, the notorious New Coke debacle was preceded by a prodigious amount of market research proving that consumers preferred the new formulation. As everyone knows, McDonald's gourmet burger miscalculation – the unforgettably named Arch Deluxe – was pre-tested till the cows came home and assured the company they were on to a winner. As everyone knows, R. J. Reynolds' calamitous brand of "smokeless" cigarettes, Premier, was backed by a money-no-object marketing campaign. But the concept was quickly stubbed out by consumers who lacked the vacuum-powered lungs needed to inhale successfully, didn't possess the pocket flame-thrower required to keep the freakin' thing alight, and couldn't acquire a taste for a fag that smelled of sulphur and, according to R. J. Reynolds' own CEO, "tasted like shit."[7]

As everyone also knows, the immortal Edsel was pimped by the best marketing muscle that Ford could afford. The name alone was pre-tested to infinity and beyond. In excess of 2,000 monikers were evaluated, including Rover, Jupiter, Arrow, Ovation, and Ariel. The poet Marianne Moore was invited to come up with a corker and she eagerly obliged, though Utopian Turtletop, Bullet Cloisonné, and Mongoose Civique didn't exactly meet with universal approval. In the end, Henry Ford opted for Edsel, even though it too failed in pre-test, and the ill-starred chrome-plated, gas-guzzling monstermobile duly sank without trace, only to resurface regularly in books about business blunders. Authors of "fail-lit" are contractually obliged to mention the Edsel.[8] Failure to do so is the recipe for fail-lit failure.

Get Out of Sale Free

Marketing, it appears, is implicated in some of the biggest business blunders on record. Virgin's god-awful cola, Harley-Davidson's fetid perfume, London's 2012 Olympics logo, Mitsubishi's much-mocked Pajero SUV ("pajero" being Spanish slang for "wanker"), and Clairol's launch of Mist Stick deodorant in Germany (rough translation: "shitstick") are just some of the many exhibits in marketing's crowded chamber of horrors.[9] And then there's gone-but-not-forgotten Fashion Café, the supermodel-supported theme restaurant that may or may not have sold Bulimic Burgers, Anorexic Shakes, and, come to think of it, offered coke in lines rather than cartons. However, it was asking for trouble with its Naomi Campbell Happy Meals ...

Disasters like these would kill off lesser management fads, fashions, or affectations. Marketing is made of sterner stuff, nevertheless. It has an escape clause on permanent retainer: namely, the oft-heard retort "You're not doing it properly!" The problem with Fashion Café wasn't marketing as such, but bad marketing! Had Clairol, Mitsubishi, Harley, or Virgin made a better fist of their marketing they wouldn't have got into the trouble that they did! Ford, R. J. Reynolds, McDonald's, and Coca-Cola were at fault because their marketing decisions were mistaken and their research effort misdirected! So there!

Marketing, according to this frequently repeated rhetorical posture, is never at fault. Marketing is content to take credit for success ("Excellent marketing campaign, chaps") but its failures are ignored, airbrushed, photoshopped, conveniently swept under the carpet ("They got it wrong. What were they thinking of?") This marketer escape clause, admittedly, is available to all management fads ("You haven't implemented six sigma as directed!"), but because modern marketing is widely if mistakenly regarded as a universal verity, it avoids the censure that descends on the quality circles, balanced scorecards, and purple cows of this world.

The gap between "ought" and "is" – what *should* be done as opposed to what's *actually* done – has long been marketing's saviour. The times they are a-changing, however. Marketing is failing and failing fast. It is teetering on the brink of oblivion. Marketing has reached what Intel supremo Andy Grove calls an "inflection point," or what others variously term "saturation," "the tipping point," "jumping the shark," and "the final countdown."

The Marketing Paradox

As with the success/failure dialectic noted in chapter 1, the principal cause of marketing's current ills is its own rude health. It is a victim of its success. It's the very ubiquity of marketing that's causing the problem. Fifty years ago, the customer-centric marketing concept conferred competitive advantage. These days, every organization is customer-oriented, or claims to be. Every start-up has embraced the marketing philosophy, if only because it's a precondition for funding by banks, venture capitalists, and their ilk. Every marketing executive has read Kotler from cover to cover, or looked at some of the pictures. Every manager is bandoliered in master's degrees, CIM diplomas, and short-course campaign medals. Every sales rep has spent many a happy weekend in CRM seminars, guerrilla-marketing bootcamps, and hug-the-customer love-ins. It is estimated that, at any one time, approximately two million people are studying marketing formally and they're all using the same textbooks, learning the same principles, working through the same syllabus. Where's the competitive advantage in that?

Terrible as Stepford textbooks, theories, and teaching programmes are, there's another even more intractable issue: everyone's a marketing expert these days. Consumers included. Fifty years ago, when Vance Packard published *The Hidden Persuaders*, many consumers were shocked (and not a little intrigued) by the mendacious machinations of marketing types. Today, they are fully *au fait* with marketers' manoeuvres and the manifold tricks of our trade. They watch TV shows about marketing and read articles in glossy magazines on brand image. They are wise to marketers' wiles, know how marketing works, appreciate that the customer is always right. They are cognizant that customer satisfaction and loyalty are the drivers of corporate competitive strategy. They can second-guess us, and we in turn must second-guess the second-guessers.

These dialectical developments, it must be acknowledged, are evident to even the most gung-ho marketing enthusiasts. Countless commentators are currently weeping, wailing, and gnashing their teeth about marketing's increasingly dire state. One apocalyptic has even announced, in a distant echo of Frederick Jackson Turner, "the closing of the marketing frontier." Only recently, the great and good of marketing academia got to grips with the issue in a book provocatively titled *Does Marketing Need Reform?* Their answer, as far as I can make out, comes from the Vicky Pollard school of scholarship, "Yeah but no but yeah but no but."[10]

So where do we go now that the marketing playing-field is level once more and everyone's a marketing expert, near enough? Who do we turn to now that innumerable indistinguishable products are available in every conceivable product category and there's only identikit, Kotlerclone, me-too marketing on offer? What do we do at a time when marketing is more important than ever (selling is easy in times of scarcity, but a bitch when abundance prevails), yet the marketing concept is stymied, stumbling, showing definite signs of mortality?

Read on, Macduff.

★ 3 ★

THE BEST OF THE WORST

There is, you'll be relieved to hear, a simple way out of marketing's current quandary. If we study those who haven't bought into conventional marketing wisdom or traditional textbook thinking, we can come up with a workable alternative to the customer-centric marketing concept. That is to say, we can learn from those who *should* have failed according to consecrated marketing principles, but who succeeded *despite* their failure to adhere to accepted principles or alleged best practice. I'm referring to people who did all right by doing it all wrong, people who are so bad they're good, people who qualify as the best of the worst.

These remarkable individuals, impertinent pen-portraits of whom will appear in the pages that follow, come from diverse walks of life, different geographical regions, and disparate historical epochs. Some of them are business people, but almost as many aren't. Granted, you may feel that today's front-line marketers have nothing to learn from a bunch of non-combatants – dead and buried non-combatants, in many cases – but marketing's own logic indicates otherwise. If, as Kotler and co. often claim, the marketing concept is applicable in every conceivable context, be it business or non-business, past or present, here, there, or everywhere, then it follows that helpful role models may be found beyond the for-profit arena, in periods prior to the present, and outside American-inspired best practice. It further follows that those of us who are looking for an alternative to prevailing marketing orthodoxy – or an inkling of an alternative, at least – are duty bound to wander off the beaten track, rummage in the dustbins of history, and study contemporary marketing mavericks such as those in the cultural industries who have no time for our obsolete textbooks, ossified theories, and obdurate thinking.

The selection process, as you'd expect from an – ahem – eminent marketing researcher like me, was nothing if not rigorous. Extensive background reading produced a 120-person list of "possibles." This was reduced to manageable proportions by multi-dimensional scaling procedures involving canonical correlation, eigenvector varimax rotation, and elimination-by-aspects analysis. The resultant model was further refined by cultural context calibration, historical epoch weightings, and for-profit/not-for-profit dummy variables. Scree tests confirm that my exemplars account for 92 percent of the variation in the original data set, at the 95 percent level of confidence. Our findings, in short, are statistically significant.

And if you believe that, brothers and sisters, you've been reading too many books by Jim Collins.[1]

Actually, my real research method – such as it is – is predicated on the approach adopted by the eminent Harvard psychologist Howard Gardner in his pioneering studies of creativity. Rejecting traditional laboratory experiments, Gardner concentrates on biographical analyses of prodigiously creative individuals (Mozart, Freud, Gandhi ...) and seeks to identify ideal types of exceptional achievement.

Oh yes, there's one last point before we start. You may be wondering why this book focuses on people rather than exemplary brands, advertising campaigns, retail stores, package designs, distribution systems, after-sales services, and the remainder of the marketing mix. It is my belief that "people" is the most important marketing "P." Advertising campaigns, package designs, and all the rest are created by people (marketers) for people (consumers), and in order to get an inkling of an alternative to the conventional marketing concept we need to look at what people do, not what traditional textbooks say. People are the alpha and omega of marketing. Behold the alpha omegas, the best of the worst, the fail incredibly betters (or FIBs for short).

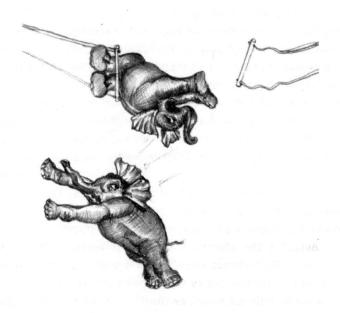

MICHAEL O'LEARY (1961–)
Ryanair's King of Mean

Michael O'Leary has a theory about failure. Businesses are on the skids, he contends, when they build themselves fancy look-at-me head offices with adjacent helicopter pads for time-pressed senior executives. They're *really* on the highway to hell, however, when the CEO writes a book disbursing nuggets of how-to wisdom. "Business books," he further opines, "are bullshit and are usually written by wankers."

Moving swiftly along, the incorrigible chief of Europe's leading low-cost airline also has a theory about global warming. Cows are to blame. Flatulent Friesians, windy Watusi, gaseous Guernseys, incontinent Charolais and their ilk are the principal cause of our present environmental crisis. Or so he claimed when faced with the uncomfortable findings of a major scientific study that said airlines' atmospheric emissions are a major contributor to global warming. Cows are much worse than jumbos, O'Leary thundered. Their carbon hoofprints are much deeper than those of the fare-paying customers Ryanair vacuum-packs into its fleet of flying cattle-trucks. The author of the hand-wringing report that condemns Ryanair and similar low-cost carriers is an "idiot economist" to boot.

Actually, the aforementioned idiot author, World Bank economist Sir Nicholas Stern, escaped pretty lightly compared to most environmentalists who cross Michael O'Leary's path. They are usually dismissed as "fuckin' lunatics." Tree-huggers in turn are treated with kid gloves compared to Ryanair's principal constituents. Travel agents are "wankers" one and all and should be "taken out and shot." The European Commission are "morons" who run "an evil empire." Merchant bankers are "fuckers" who "piss away money." Airport operators, BAA in particular, are "overcharging rapists." The Air Traffic Users

Committee is "a bunch of half-wits." The UK government's anti-terrorist measures at airports are straight out of "the Keystone Cops." Britain's air traffic control system is not only "poxy" but "a fucking shambles." Rival airlines are variously described as "a dog," "a platoon of goons," "a shitty operator on shitty routes," "a bunch of swindlers," or, bizarrely, "not the brightest sandwich in the picnic." And as for the Irish government, which has repeatedly attempted to hamper Ryanair's rapid expansion, I can only leave O'Leary's comments to your fevered four-lettered imagination.[2]

The Mouth from Mullingar reserves his extra-special ire for customers, however. Never let it be said that O'Leary is a closet customer-coddler. On the contrary, he's the "Chainsaw" Al Dunlap of customer care. Whatever you do, don't ask for a refund, because a kick in the knackers can offend. Don't ask for Air Miles, because you'll get a foot, with a boot, right up your bony ass. Don't ask for a wheelchair, because getting up the steps unassisted is a bugger. Don't ask for an airport convenient to your destination, because that isn't on the company's customer charter. Don't win a "free flights for life" competition, as Ryanair's millionth passenger did, because you'll have trouble getting a seat, let alone a glass of champagne. Don't ask for a free transfer to a later flight, not even for a family bereavement, because it ain't gonna happen without an eye-watering surcharge (think ozone-sized hole in your wallet). Don't ask for in-flight meals, generous baggage allowances, tastefully appointed departure lounges, or complimentary sick bags, because what are you, some kind of wimp? Don't ask for a pre-assigned seat, much less a reclinable one with adequate legroom, because you're lucky you've got a seat, amigo. Sharp spikes are on order, awaiting CAA approval. Don't even ask for an aircraft, compadre, because if operational reasons dictate that a plane's unavailable, you're on your own. As are your travelling companions, be they disabled children, doddery grandparents, or demented relatives.

Ryanair isn't called Aer O'Flot for nothing, you know.

Michael O'Leary may have re-engineered customer orientation, but there's no denying his company's outstanding success. Ryanair's relentless focus on lowering costs extends to charging for check-in facilities, for God's sake. Its Savonarola-like determination to eschew services or overcharge for the few it provides is genuinely frightening. Its Jesuitical desire to pummel prices while whipping up profits, thanks to a merciless yield-management–driven website, is the nearest thing to flagellation this side of Opus Dei. Its brilliant ability to maximize operational efficiencies – by means of the 45-minute turnaround, interchangeable fleet of easily maintained aircraft, avoidance of hub-and-spoke for a point-to-point network, *et cetera* – is sufficient to ensure that Ryanair is the most profitable operator in its sector, if not the world. Far from being an aggressive upstart, a puny David battling the price-gouging Goliaths of commercial aviation, Ryanair is the undisputed champion of fight and flight, the biggest bully in the business. It's the airline that every consumer loves to hate, hate, and hate again.

If there's one thing O'Leary likes even less than whingeing, moaning, never-done-complaining customers, it's brand consultants, marketing experts, and analogous "bolloxologists." His idea of a marketing makeover is to treat the sides of his aircraft as advertising hoardings or to perform cosmetic surgery on Ryanair's logo, an anthropomorphic harp whose breasts he augmented from circa C-cup to DD or thereabouts. Yet for all his adherence to the Pamela Anderson school of brand image enhancement, O'Leary is no slouch when it comes to publicity stunts. He infuriated the Vatican by claiming that the Pope's Easter message concerned Ryanair's devilishly low fares. Cue copious free publicity. He infuriated the Airline Pilots' Association by contending that hijackers would have to go a long way to get lower fares than Ryanair's. Cue copious free publicity. He infuriated the Advertising Standards Authority with a Valentine's Day special, priced at a suggestive £69, featuring the breathtaking strapline "Well, blow me." Cue copious free publicity. He infuriated rival operator British Airways with an attack ad describing them as "expensive bastards." Cue copious free publicity, especially when BA sued, only to lose the case because the judge concluded they really *were* expensive bastards. He infuriated another competing airline by leading a guerrilla attack on their headquarters, complete with fully operational Sherman tank, platoon of fatigues-wearing foot soldiers, and marching song composed for the occasion: "I've been told and it's no lie/EasyJet's fares are way too high." Cue ... you know what.

Never reluctant, in fact, to wear a uniform, Colonel O'Leary has variously dressed up as Santa Claus, the Easter Bunny, a swashbuckling pirate, a cigar-chomping Winston Churchill wannabe, a motormouth Trappist monk, and – in an outfit worn on sufficient occasions to make one wonder – a frilly-knickered French maid. *Oh la la*. Oh O'Leary. Never mind the column inches, Michael, feel the lacy material.

Richard Branson, BTW, is also fond of the French maid look. But his legs aren't as good as O'Leary's.

Still, for all his OTT antics, the really interesting thing about the cult of Michael O'Leary is the massive disjunction between persona and person. He presents himself as an ill-educated hick from the sticks who plays football with the baggage handlers, eats beans 'n' chips in the staff canteen, and swears like a Tourette's-afflicted hoodie from Asboville. He dresses in a farm-labourer ensemble, aspires to own a couple of country pubs, disdains the chardonnay-quaffing chattering classes, and makes much of his down-to-earth upbringing in the market town of Mullingar. However, the O'Leary reality is that he's a "highly educated, gently reared scion of Irish country aristocrats."[3] He was schooled at Ireland's Eton, Clongowes Wood College (James Joyce's alma mater), read business studies at Ireland's Oxbridge, Trinity College, Dublin, and worked for a blue-chip accountancy practice, Stokes

Kennedy Crowley, before becoming Ryanair's financial enforcer. He lives in a palatial stately home, Gigginstown House, where he runs a stable of thoroughbred racehorses including Economy Drive and War of Attrition. He has an acclaimed art collection, owns a villa or two in Italy, is a regular patron of exclusive Dublin eateries, and, far from being a Celtic Che Guevara, is a bit of a mummy's boy, apparently.

But don't tell him I said that.

Michael O'Leary, in sum, is an inscrutable individual. He is a working-class hero with a silver spoon in his mouth. He loathes the media circus but is a PR ringmaster of rare ability. He treats his customers diabolically – although not nearly as diabolically as he treats his suppliers – and they keep coming back for more. He comes across as a flamboyant, finagling flim-flam man, to put it politely, yet his company's accounting practices are extremely conservative and each competitive move is carefully calculated. He has had failures aplenty (a fair proportion of Ryanair's new routes fail to take off and are quickly axed), but his successes are second to none. He has no time for full-of-it marketing types, yet for many if not most consumers he typifies the full-of-it marketing type. He's Wal-Mart with wings.

SAM WALTON (1918–92)
Hix from the Styx

The Styx, in Greek mythology, is one of the underworld's nine rivers. On the far side, the three-headed guard dog Cerberus prowls menacingly. Damn that genetically modified Pedigree Chum! On the near side stands Charon, the hard-bargaining ferryman-cum-*maître d'*. Not just anyone can get into Hades, much less command a corner table. Certainly not the likes of you 'n' me.

There's more to the Styx than getting past doorbitches, however. Just like a visit to Lourdes, Leamington Spa, or Champneys, a dip in the Styx can do wonders for some and confer immortality on others. According to legend, Achilles was submerged therein, though he was held by the heel that proved his undoing.

So it is with Wal-Mart. No, they're not planning a Super-center on the outskirts of Hades, thereby destroying the diabolical downtown, bankrupting satanic small businesses, and doing untold long-term damage to the infernal environment. They're negotiating for a suitable site, though.

Sam Walton, rather, is the Achilles of Wal-Mart. A store-keeping superhero, he had a fatal flaw in his marketing makeup. Achilles-like, he's also wrapped in several layers of legend and company lore. The eldest son of a repo man – business was booming in the Midwest during the Great Depression, as you can imagine – Sam showed his entrepreneurial prowess at an early age. He sold milk from the family farm, hawked magazine subscriptions, threw numerous newspaper rounds, and was known as "Hustler" Walton at college. He joined J. C. Penney on graduation, only to be belittled by his line manager with the immortal words, "Maybe you're just not cut out for retail, son."[4]

Undeterred, Sam decided to become a department store co-owner in St Louis. His wife, however, refused to go. Helen was a country girl at heart. She didn't want to raise her kids in the big bad city, a decision that was to have profound consequences because it determined the strategic focus of the behemoth to come. So, stymied by his spouse – and bankrolled by his father-in-law – Walton took on a Ben Franklin variety-store franchise in the small town of Newport, Arkansas. It took off like the proverbial scalded cat, thanks in no small part to Walton's dubious buying practices (which broke his legally binding franchise agreement), hubba-hubba promotional abilities (ice-cream machine on the sidewalk, four pairs of polyester panties for $1), and utterly ruthless determination to destroy the competition (purchasing a store across the street to prevent his principal rival expanding, for example).

After five years of small-town success, Sam struck out. His lease was up and he'd failed to secure an option to renew. The owner of the property promptly acquired the business that workaholic Walton had painstakingly put together. Denied! Older but wiser, the retail neophyte moved to an even smaller Arkansas town, Bentonville, where he opened an eponymous five-and-dime that paved the way for the first Wal-Mart proper in 1962. Bar an inept attempt to dabble in property development, Sam never looked back.

Part of the first post-war wave of self-service discount stores, Wal-Mart had the Midwest pretty much to itself. Despite leading brand-name companies' refusal to supply him, a severe shortage of suitable store managers, and stiff competition from traditional small-town mom-and-pop shops, Walton built up his organization outlet by outlet, county by county, state by state. By the time the company was listed on the NYSE on 31 October 1969, it had 32 stores in five states, employed 1,500 people, and generated sales of $50 million or thereabouts.

Today, Wal-Mart is the biggest retailer in the world and the second-largest corporation after Exxon Mobil. With annual sales of $351 billion, 6,000 or so retail establishments, subsidiary operations in Argentina, Brazil, Puerto Rico, Mexico (Walmex), Great Britain (Asda), and Japan (Sieyu) – don't mention the war Wal-Mart lost in Germany or the recent retreat from South Korea – and no fewer than 1.9 million employees, Wal-Mart is mega. It boggles the mind. Not only has it taken over the world, it's sizing up the underworld, as we have seen. Heaven can wait.

Much has been written about the serial category-killer from Bentonville. It wasn't incorporated on Hallowe'en for nothing. The raptor of retail, Wal-Mart's success has been attributed to its ferocious frugality, ruthless cost-cutting, baleful bargaining power, nefarious store-opening strategies, and frighteningly efficient logistics, goods-handling, and merchandise-replenishment procedures, to say nothing of its rabidly enthusiastic employees (sorry, "associates"), disconcertingly sunny "greeters" (originally introduced as a deterrent to shoplifters), and monomaniacal managerial dedication to sweating every asset (and those of its suppliers for good measure). Then there's that creepy satellite-based surveillance system that's just like the CIA's, FBI's, and NSA's, only better.

All of these traits, from airborne surveillance to everyday low pricing, are the sons of Sam. For all his folksy, down-home, plain-spoken, aw-shucks, gee-whiz, one-of-the-boys, cornball-from-Hayseed-City, God-bless-America-the-Beautiful demeanour – read his autobiography and barf – Uncle Sam Walton was a hard-driving, penny-pinching, gimlet-eyed, brook-no-opposition, bottom-line-obsessed operator. He was an information maven, moreover, who was not only willing to learn from anyone but prepared to implement ideas, however fanciful, with Achilles-like alacrity. Failure didn't bother Sam in the slightest, because unworkable ideas could be abandoned as quickly as they were adopted. Unlike the other discounters that emerged in the early 1960s (Kmart especially), Wal-Mart never succumbed to ossified thinking, cruise-control conservatism, or fat-cat featherbedding, or indeed displayed anything other than a burning desire to be the best of the best. In fact, Wal-Mart's gourmand-oid expansion in the 1980s and 1990s was fed by discount-retailer roadkill. There was no shortage of chainstore carrion back then.

Voracious it may have been, but the buzzard from Bentonville had another feather in its baseball cap: marketing. Make no mistake, Mr Sam was a marketer of genius. Granted, he didn't get off to a very good start. The grand opening of his first store in Harrison featured free watermelons and donkey rides. But it was an extremely hot day. The melons popped, the donkeys pooped, and the resultant mulch was tramped through the store by swarming shoppers. Had he bottled the malodorous aroma, Sam could've given Skunk Guard a run for its money.

Failed experiments in retail atmospherics aside, Sam Walton was the Wonderful Wizard of Ozarks. He famously performed a hula on Wall Street, complete with leis, grass skirt, tropical shirt, and ukulele-strumming backing band. His store managers and senior executives, what's more, repeatedly pulled off goofy attention-grabbing marketing stunts: bear wrestling, bareback riding, pig calling, moon pie eating contests, drag-queen competitions (don't go there, *mes amis*), and outback awaydays for stockbrokers, financial analysts, and similar city slickers. Better yet was his "Buy American" campaign of the mid-1980s, a PR triumph at a time when Wal-Mart was offshoring its own-label apparel suppliers like they were going out of fashion. Sam even turned his status as America's richest man to promotional advantage, since his frugal lifestyle – battered overalls, beat-up pickup truck, $5 haircuts, *et al.* – served as an admirable old-fashioned counterpoint to the mindless consumerism of the "greed is good" decade. Mindless consumerism, it must be said, that Wal-Mart exacerbated with its unbelievably low prices and conveniently countrywide coverage.

Crass and corny though it was, Wal-Mart's Midwestern marketing worked. But it didn't work as well as Mr Sam's internal marketing. Hustler Walton's most brilliant marketing achievements were reserved for his associates. Sales meetings, supplier conventions, store visits, stockholder seminars, company newsletters, CCTV broadcasts, annual results announcements, and, above all, the legendary Saturday morning powwows for senior managers were unfailingly imbued with ra-ra razzamatazz. Celebrities dropped in, prizes were awarded, skits were performed, and the cheerleader-in-chief rallied the troops with company chants. Give me a W. Give me an A. Give me an L. Give me a squiggly. Never has a hyphen induced so much grotesque gyration among obese Middle Americans. Try not to think about it. The chant, naturally, climaxed with Walton shouting "Who's Number One?" And the workers yelled back, "The customer!"

The customer, of course, was never Number One. Wal-Mart was Number One. Number One was all it ever wanted to be, and since Sam's death in 1992, the company has perpetuated his top-dog ambition. As numerous trade unionists and small-town retailers can testify, Cerberus is a chihuahua by comparison.

EDWARD L. BERNAYS (1891–1995)
Baron of Ballyhoo

Fooled us, they did. Laura and Jim. Kinda disappointed by their behaviour. We thought they were travellin' coast-to-coast in a crappy camper van. Stopping every night in the handiest Wal-Mart parking lot. That's the impression they gave in their folksy travel blog, *Wal-Marting Across America*. Yeah, guess we shoulda realized that their encounters with kindly Wal-Mart employees, all spoutin' heart-warming stories about their truly wunnerful employer, were jest too good to be true. But the blog seemed so authentic that we kinda fell fer it. Turns out Wal-Mart's PR company, Edelman, was behind Laura 'n' Jim. Turns out Edelman's behind a lot of phoney-baloney blogs, such as *Working Families for Wal-Mart*, which outs trades union activists bent on dissin' the carin' sharin' retail chain.[5] Turns out there are a lot of blogs that flog out there in cyberspace. Turns out lotsa companies are gettin' in on Edelman's act: Coca-Cola, Captain Morgan's Rum, and McDonald's, whose "Mike" claimed to have found a French fry shaped like Abe Lincoln. Turns out you *can* fool a lot of the people a lot of the time.

Consumers, of course, should know better than to fall for a "flog." The technique's as old as the hills. It was perfected in the 1920s by Edward L. Bernays, PR man nonpareil. Variously described as the Prince of Puff, the Pontiff of Publicity, the Baron of Ballyhoo, and the Father of Public Relations, Bernays' modus operandi involved behind-the-scenes manoeuvres.[6] Typically, he formed an "impartial" committee on matters pertaining to the client's "cause," peopled it with open-minded members of the great and the good, generated copious press coverage of the disinterested committee's even-handed deliberations, and kept his string-pulling hidden at all times. He was a master of manipulation, a Svengali of the smokescreen, an advocate of corporate social irresponsibility. His policy wasn't to respond to consumer needs or desires, but to change their behaviour *en masse*, without them being any the wiser. He wrote the book on (and called) *Propaganda*, a well-thumbed copy of which was owned by one Joseph Goebbels. He believed that marketers should make the multitudes do as they're bid by whatever means necessary. He subscribed to the view subsequently articulated by McDonald's head honcho, Ray Kroc: "Salesmanship is the art of letting the customer have it your way." Bernays was more forthright, however. He called this "the engineering of consent."

Nowhere is Bernays' method – an approach he termed "appeals of indirection" – better illustrated than in his work on books, bacon, and bananas. The publishers Harcourt Brace had their books promoted not by a conventional PR campaign, but by the simple expedient of encouraging architects, contractors, and decorators to add built-in bookshelves to their property developments. Wherever there are bookshelves, Bernays reasoned, there will be books. Analogously, when a leading American bacon producer called Beechnut Packing was in a tizzy about falling sales thanks to the growing popularity of Kellogg's breakfast cereals, Bernays organized a campaign to change the nation's eating habits. Leading medical authorities were surveyed about the benefits of hearty breakfasts. They concurred that bigger was better. Newspapers were appraised of the medics' informed opinion, sales of bacon and eggs soared, and the full American breakfast was born. Conversely, when bizarre rumours started to circulate about bananas causing polio, Bernays was hired by the United Fruit Company. Rather than have the company refute the rumours directly, which wouldn't have been believed and would only have lent credibility to the unfounded allegations, PR's top banana persuaded a front organization, the National Foundation for Infantile Paralysis, to run a rumour-dispelling advertising campaign. The promotion was surreptitiously underwritten by UFC, the NFIP benefited from the free publicity, and, most important of all, Bernays was retained by UFC thereafter. At enormous expense.

Be that as it may, the Baron of Ballyhoo's work on the Lucky Strike cigarette account was even more insidious, and puts Edelman's Wal-Mart flog to shame. He was responsible for the "Torches of Freedom" parade, a widely publicized, supposedly spontaneous protest march by emancipated women against the taboo on smoking outdoors. Lucky Strike just happened to be targeted at female smokers, a huge and largely untapped market. Bernays followed "Torches" with the legendary "Reach for a Lucky instead of a sweet" campaign, which again involved ostensibly impartial medical authorities recommending cigarettes' appetite-suppressing, waistline-preserving abilities and their all-round contribution to a healthy diet. Bernays even managed to make green the nation's favourite colour thanks to a star-studded Emerald Ball, a cascade of green-related stories in newspapers, and a series of learned lectures on the place of the colour in western art and culture. Lucky Strike's livery just happened to be green as well.

Brilliant through it was, Bernays' greening of America pales beside his Edison anniversary achievements. Celebrated in October 1929, the fiftieth anniversary of electric light was the very model of a modern public relations campaign. For a full year beforehand, the newspapers were filled with Bernays-planted Edisonalia. These included unprompted "letters of tribute" from the likes of Albert Einstein and all sorts of special sections, souvenir reprints, and cut-out-and-keepsakes. Legendary songwriter George M. Cohan was persuaded to dash off a ditty entitled "Edison the miracle man" and encouraged to belt it out at every available opportunity. Such was the outpouring of totally spontaneous public adoration – well, OK, totally drummed-up public adoration – that a commemorative stamp was issued by the US Postal Service, a hitherto unheard-of honour. The golden jubilee climaxed with a five-day festival at

Edison's celebrated Menlo Park laboratory, where a resplendent roster of national dignitaries (President Herbert Hoover,
Marie Curie, Orville Wright, Henry Ford, and so forth) assembled to re-enact the legendary "let there be light" moment for
the newsreels, radio stations, newspaper reporters, and spe-
cially invited guests. The honours were performed by the
imperishable inventor himself, tempted out of retirement at
the grand old age of 82. "Mr Edison," NBC's radio reporter
whispered reverentially, "has the two wires in his hand. Now
he is reaching up to the old lamp. Now he is making the connection. It lights!"

Light's golden jubilee was a PR triumph, and a triumph
for Edward Bernays in particular. Even though his role was
largely advisory, he managed to garner much of the credit.
Indeed, for all his energy, efficiency, ability, and astuteness –
not to mention his sterling work for a host of blue-chip clients
from General Motors to Procter & Gamble – Eddie's eye for the
main chance was unerring. When all is said and done, his
biggest client was himself, and he promoted his biggest client
relentlessly. Indeed, if his 850-page autobiography is to be
believed, he was personally responsible for women's liberation,
the state of Israel, making beer America's beverage of choice,
instituting the interstate highway system, ensuring the election of Calvin Coolidge, and establishing the reputation of,
among others, Enrico Caruso, Ballets Russes, and his little-
known Austrian uncle, Sigmund Freud.[7]

Suffice to say, the veracity of these extravagant claims has
been debated at length, as has his involvement in the Guatema-
lan coup of 1954, when CIA-backed rebels overthrew the demo-
cratically elected government at the behest of the United Fruit
Company. What is not in doubt is that Bernays was the foremost self-publicist in an industry untroubled by shy and retiring types. He even managed to persuade posterity that he
founded the PR profession, conveniently overlooking his celebrated predecessors (most notably Ivy Lee). His reputation,

however, owes much to the fact that he long outlived his contemporaries, who thus weren't around to dispute his spin on the spin-doctoring business. His monumental memoirs, numerous books on PR practice, and massive Library of Congress bequest comprising 800 boxes of private and professional papers also helped keep his memory green among the marketing community, as he knew they would. The mere fact that he appears in every anthology of marketing giants, when there are others equally deserving but absent, speaks volumes for his marketing brilliance. He won't worm his way into this book, though. No way, Bernays.

JOSEPH DUVEEN (1869–1939)
The Lovable Buccaneer

Some sales are tougher to make than others. Some, like the Airbus 380, are very tough indeed. Art, however, is arguably the toughest of all. Great works of art, Old Masters in particular, are inordinately expensive unnecessary objects. They are the ultimate non-essential. A half-decent art collection is considerably more expensive than wardrobes full of haute couture, or the glittering creations of bespoke jewellers, or even otiose acquisitions of Premiership soccer clubs.

Selling Old Masters is the supreme marketing challenge. Selling Old Masters to penny-pinching plutocrats is more challenging still. Yet that is the market Joseph Duveen dominated for years. He was the greatest art dealer ever.[8]

The eldest of twelve children, Joseph Duveen was a Hull-bred Yorkshireman. His father, an eager 1866 arrival from Amsterdam, was a small-time Delft dealer who graduated to an upmarket furniture showroom in Oxford Street, London. From an early age, Joseph was spoon-fed with information on the operation of the shop. He ran errands, arranged stock, wrapped packages, and studied the subtleties of his father's sales technique, especially when moneyed customers called. One day, an obviously affluent couple with pronounced Irish accents appeared on the premises and started buying ornamental screens with gusto. Duveen slipped outside, generously tipped the waiting coachman and extracted the extravagant arrivals' name, which he quietly conveyed to his father. When the sated aristocrats turned to the shopkeeper with the words "You must be wondering why we're buying so many screens," Duveen's father replied, "Not at all, Lady Guinness, you have many fine houses and you are quite right to supply them with screens." Delighted at being recognized, the

Guinnesses became loyal customers thereafter, as did their aristocratic acquaintances.

On his father's death in 1906, Duveen took over the family firm as his siblings weren't especially commercially minded. By this stage, Duveen had established an enviable reputation as the coming man in art dealing. He had paid record sums for two major collections, those of Oskar Hainauer and Rodolphe Kann, which he broke up and sold off as single items – in art as elsewhere, infinitely more profitable than job lots. More important, the astonishing financial outlay required to purchase the two collections created a buzz around the art world that more than justified the investment. It made Duveen's name. And name is all in art dealing.

Duveen, then, was acutely aware of the rhetoric of big numbers. His paintings were always the most expensive on the market. His outlay on acquisitions was the biggest in the trade by far. He bid record-breaking prices for artists such as Rembrandt, whose work he already possessed in abundance. The inevitable upshot was that the new record price soon became the base price for all Rembrandts, and the worth of his pre-existing holdings increased immeasurably. When a collection was dispersed, moreover, Duveen not only bought back the pieces he'd previously sold to the collector, but bid the prices up to ensure that the value of "Duveens" never went down. Or, more precisely, were never seen to go down. He thereby established the principle that there are many Old Masters but only one Duveen. Old Masters handled by the master dealer are far superior to just any old Old Masters. Paintings appreciated on association with the divine Duveen. All else was mere wall-covering.

A master self-publicist at a time when déclassé art dealers embraced anonymity, Duveen was described as an "exalted middleman." He oozed affluence. He owned palatial homes crammed with high-calibre masterworks. His galleries in London, Paris, and New York were made from the finest construction materials and finished to a standard commensurate with the priceless works of art they contained. He was not averse to disparaging the paintings handled by rival dealers, or insinuating that they were fakes. "I smell fresh paint" was one of his favourite put-downs, though it triggered numerous suits for defamation. The resultant court cases only added to his stellar reputation as the dealer to deal with. When he acquired Gainsborough's *The Blue Boy* for the Californian railroad magnate H. E. Huntington, it was placed on display in London prior to departure. The attend-ant national lamentation over the loss of an irreplaceable English treasure was music to the ears of Huntington and Duveen alike. When the much-publicized painting finally arrived in New York, the "loveable buccaneer" refused to display it in the Met, because the gimcrack museum wasn't good enough for Gainsborough's masterpiece. Cole Porter, no less, was moved to write a song about the episode, the lyrics of which namechecked delightful, delicious, de-lovely Duveen.

Self-promotion may have been part of Duveen's marketing strategy, but only a small part. The key to his staggering success was his sublime sales technique. His customers, remember, were multi-multi-millionaires who'd made their vast fortunes at the zenith of American red-in-tooth-and-claw capi-talism: J. P. Morgan, John D. Rockefeller, Henry Clay Frick, Andrew Mellon, and numerous names long since forgotten but greatly esteemed at the time. These people were not naïve financially, nor unfamiliar with the patter of salespeople. Most were preternaturally parsimonious, having been small shop-keepers or street-smart hustlers or hard-scrabble farmers before becoming self-made men. Yet Duveen got them to spend staggering amounts of money on utterly unnecessary fripper-ies. How did he do it?

First, he refused to sell to them. Whatever artwork they wanted, it was invariably unavailable, part of Duveen's private collection, something he simply couldn't bear to part with. Duveen dangled the beautiful bait in front of them, described its insuperable qualities at length, and then refused to let the painting go. Thus they wanted it all the more.

Second, he intimated that the painting was being kept for another collector, an exceptionally eminent one who was prepared to pay a vast price for the immemorial artefact. By adding an element of competition to the acquisitive urge – and competition was catnip to the lions of turn-of-the-century American society – Duveen ensured that their desire to buy was off the scale.

Third, he insinuated that clients weren't good enough for the works under consideration, that their powers of discrimination were insufficiently developed to appreciate the ineffable masterpiece. You are not worthy, he implied. Come back to me when you have the taste, refinement, perspicacity, and indeed setting to deserve the artwork in question.

Duveen, in fact, often scrutinized his prospects' possessions to see if they were of sufficient calibre to accommodate the priceless item he was holding. How could he entrust them with a Rembrandt or Titian or Giotto if it would be surrounded by low-grade tat? As luck would have it, he had other pieces that, if purchased, could create conditions conducive to the eventual arrival of an immortal. Once upon a time, none other than William Randolph Hearst – newspaper mogul and model for Orson Welles' *Citizen Kane* – wished to avail himself of Duveen's munificence. The dealer's dealer picked his way through the tycoon's peerless collection shaking his head in sorrow. When shown San Simeon's *pièce de résistance*, an exquisite pair of Rossellino angels:

> Duveen made a barely audible remark that cast doubt on their legitimacy, then left ... There was a sad interval after his departure; Hearst was like a college boy who, after cramming hard for an exam, has the terrible feeling that he's flunked it. He was suddenly seized by a devastating doubt about everything he had. He shouted despairingly to Mrs Hearst, "If those angels aren't right, then nothing is right!"[9]

Alongside his mastery of reverse psychology, Duveen was a virtuoso of the free gift. He disbursed gratuities like they were going out of style. Apart from his enormous emoluments to the nation, such as the Elgin Marbles room at the British Museum and the Modern Foreign galleries at the Tate, he doled out prodigious tips to clients' valets, butlers, and other servants, as well as rival galleries' employees. He offered no-charge services for well-heeled customers – restoration, storage, authentication, irreplaceable objects on extended approval – arranged entrées into high society for his gauche American squillionaires, and took prospects on personally conducted tours of museums, galleries, stately homes, royal palaces, and suchlike, all of which reinforced his reputation as a man of monumental means, impeccable breeding, and singular influence. He made up gift catalogues for individual clients: exquisitely bound, beautifully illustrated volumes itemizing all their Duveen-supplied paintings, along with a crystalline summary of each artwork's impeccable provenance. These extremely expensive catalogues were presented gratis to his very best customers. But boy, did they repay the investment.

Duveen understood better than anyone that free gifts come with social obligations and must be reciprocated. The services to a grateful nation were rewarded with a peerage. The well-tipped servants supplied crucial market intelligence. The clients who availed themselves of, say, his free room design or no-charge wedding services duly bought their furnishings or wedding presents from the majestic middleman. The customers who kept goods on extended approval couldn't bear to see them go when their time was up. (The prices had also gone up in the interim, in direct proportion to customers' ownership urges.) The personally guided tours of stately homes just happened to be stately homes with heirlooms for sale – ones that Duveen had first dibs on. The free catalogues not only stimulated purchases from recipients, but because they were given only to Duveen's *very best* clients, they also stimulated purchases among those non-recipients who aspired to very best client status.

A final quality that Duveen had in abundance was enthusiasm. An ebullient, exuberant, incessantly effervescent individual with seemingly boundless energy, Duveen was as garrulous about art as they come. Although he played the part of a diffident, slightly dotty, stereotypically English gentleman, his enthusiasm in the presence of great art was infectious. Having convinced himself that a work was wonderful, he could convince everyone else too. "The pictures," Andrew Mellon once ruefully observed to the indefatigable dealer, "always look better when you are here."

Wonder what he'd make of Tracey Emin?

LOLA MONTEZ (1821–61)
Along Came a Spider

If marketers retail what Donald Trump calls "truthful hyper-bole," then Lola Montez must qualify as one of the greatest marketers of all time. Some thought she was Spanish. Others assumed she was Scottish. Many believed she was born in India. Most suspected she was a genuine Bavarian countess. Everyone, however, had heard of this wicked, wicked woman.[10] In the 1840s, she was the most famous female in the world after Queen Victoria, far ahead of contemporary luminaries like Fanny Elssler, Jenny Lind, and Florence Nightingale. Her public lectures even outdrew those of Charles Dickens, who was big, big, big back then and no slouch in the self-marketing stakes either.

Lola eclipsed them all. Born in Sligo, Ireland, Eliza Gilbert came from an illegitimate branch of a prominent Protestant family. She was brought up in India, where her father died of cholera, her teenage mother soon remarried, and the newly-weds sent the skittish youngster back to the UK for a proper British upbringing. Eliza wasn't best pleased. She started exhibiting the tempestuous streak that characterized her later life. Adolescence exacerbated her volatility and she was shipped off to an exclusive boarding school for well-bred young women in Bath, then a fashionable resort for blue bloods, where she blossomed into a stunningly beautiful, extremely well educated ingénue, with no conception of her impact on the opposite sex. Foolishly, she fell for one Lieutenant Thomas James, a thirty-year-old acquaintance of her mother, promptly eloped with the Irish rapscallion, married him in Dublin and settled down to a life of mind-boggling monotony in the windy wilds of Wexford.

When a chance to return to India arose, Eliza leaped at the

opportunity. Unfortunately, the close confinement of the long journey destroyed what little affection existed between the middle-aged soldier and his rapidly maturing child bride. After coping as best she could with the mosquito-plagued privations of army life on the North Indian Plain, she abandoned her abusive husband and fled to her mother in Calcutta. Her mother didn't want to know, and the nineteen-year-old was shipped, yet again, back to Britain. En route, she scandalized the captain and crew of the good ship *Larkins* by consorting with a well-connected young aristocrat, Lieutenant George Lennox. Eliza was already a social outcast, given her earlier elopement and failed marriage, but her unchaperoned dalliance with Lt Lennox was way, way beyond the pale. The ultimate sanction was applied: exclusion from the captain's table.

Worse was to come. Eliza established a love nest with Lennox in London, snubbed the Irish and Scottish relatives who tried to save her from perdition, and, when the steamy affair had run its course, found herself on the receiving end of a writ from her estranged husband, Lt James. He was suing for divorce, an action that guaranteed social death and an irrecoverably lost reputation back then.

What to do? An untouchable in 1840s England, with nary a ha'penny to her tainted name, the ex-Mrs James was in serious trouble. But she was incredibly pretty and nothing if not feisty. So she reinvented herself as an exotic dancer – the ravishing Spanish beauty Lola Montez. She also managed to bluff her way onto the bill of Victorian London's pre-eminent venue, Her Majesty's Theatre, where she was showcased as an intermission act during a command performance of *The Barber of Seville*. Ms Montez, bear in mind, had no previous training as a danseuse, none whatsoever. She had never appeared on a stage before, let alone the most prestigious stage in the Empire, at the height of the London season, with everyone who was anyone in attendance, royalty and nobility included. All Lola had to offer was stunning beauty, wonderfully expressive features, an extremely well-turned ankle, and a self-choreographed routine that, um, displayed her talents to their best advantage.

The balmy evening of 3 June 1843 witnessed the first performance of Montez's legendary spider dance. This routine, if you can call it that, was based on the premise that a tarantula had somehow inveigled itself into Lola's undergarments and was running riot as the artiste endeavoured to extricate it from her unmentionables. The rampaging arachnid forced the unfortunate dancer to raise her skirts higher and higher as the performance progressed, until, at the climactic moment, she removed the invisible brute from her scanties, cast it to the ground, and crushed the sucker underfoot. Phew, that was close!

Pandemonium reigned, as you can imagine. It reigned for several nights thereafter. It reigned even harder when Mrs James's true background leaked out, though she vociferously denied allegations about her murky marital escapades. It reigned throughout Europe as Lola took her is-that-a-spider-in-your-petticoat-or-are-you-just-pleased-to-show-me? routine on the road, adding several new dances to her repertoire, all minor variations on the spider.

The incessant touring wasn't good for Lola's equanimity, however. She fought with Prussian cavalry officers, she punched out upstart hoteliers, she soundly thrashed chiselling stage managers, she set about anyone who cast aspersions on her artistic abilities. Her temper was terrible too. Notoriety, nevertheless, has never been bad for business in the cultural industries. And the scandalous Spanish dancer certainly knew how to draw a crowd. Upbraided as a bad influence on public morals, she was banished from several Central European cities including Berlin, Warsaw, and Baden-Baden. Whenever she wasn't performing, furthermore, she found sufficient love-struck admirers to keep her in the style to which she was rapidly becoming accustomed. She had a tempestuous affair with Liszt, took a rich lover in Paris who fought a duel on her behalf – fatal mistake – and eventually turned up at the Royal Court Theatre in Munich. Then the real fun started.

King Ludwig I, the diligent, much-loved, hard-working, penny-pinching, 50-year-old ruler of Bavaria, saw the Spanish temptress perform during Oktoberfest 1846. He fell for her big time. He lavished jewels, horses, houses, gifts, portraits, citizenship, and even a royal title, Countess of Landsfeldt, upon the object of his unquenchable desire.

Understandably, the honest burghers of Bavaria were outraged, especially when Lola let it be known that she had the king under her thumb, that she called the shots in his court, and that her supporters would receive preferential treatment when it came to royal appointments and the like. She also surrounded herself with a gaggle of handsome young men, who not only partied hard with the shameless hussy but egged her on to ever more outrageous acts: tongue-lashing shopkeepers, horsewhipping soldiers on guard duty, slapping police officers about a bit, and refusing to curtsey in the presence of His Royal Highness.

Riots broke out. Martial law was declared. Lola was run out of town with a lover or two in tow. The infatuated king eventually abdicated over the shocking episode, every embarrassing detail of which was splashed over every newspaper in the civilized world. And also in America.

Fresh from her conquest of Bavaria, the countess set sail for the United States. Her ever-trusty spider dance went down a storm, especially in California, where the gold miners didn't get to see too many beautiful women, let alone a creature as stunning as Lola. To give the temptress her due, Ms Montez worked hard to improve her stagecraft and, with a hand-picked repertory company behind her, she acquitted herself admirably in various theatrical standards, such as Sheridan's seminal *School for Scandal*. Not that she had much to learn about schooling scandal.

Having barnstormed the USA, and having found herself

another sugar daddy, Lola set sail for Australia with her repertory players for company. The gold miners in Victoria were as enamoured as their Californian counterparts, though they let themselves down by drowning out the warm-up acts with chants of "Spider, spider, spider." They know a thing or two about spiders in the Antipodes, and Lola didn't disappoint. Her touring company wasn't so happy, however. They had the Montez scars, Montez bite-marks, and Montez horsewhip wheals to prove it.

When her sugar daddy disappeared overboard on the voyage home – I'm not making this up – Lola reinvented herself yet again, this time as a lecturer on the public-speaking circuit. She toured the world delivering homilies on beauty, love, politics, American society, the iniquities of the Roman Catholic Church, and how she had done more for female emancipation than the harridans who led the then-burgeoning women's movement, which was true. As with all of her theatrical performances, Lola charged premium prices for the lectures, often three or four times the norm, and had no trouble filling sizeable amphitheatres for weeks at a time. She also published several bestselling books on beauty, masculinity, and human relationships. She wasn't lacking in experience by that stage. Naturally, she was denounced wherever she went, but such was her wanton reputation that she never wanted for anything. Her monumental rages were counterbalanced by acts of incredible generosity, as well as lashings of Irish charm, Spanish sultriness, Indian allure, Bavarian belligerence, and Scottish grit. Quite a combination. Quite a woman. Quite a marketer. Olé.

MARVIN BOWER (1903–2003)
Firm Foundation

Straight-talkers, by and large, are full of shit. Forgive my candour, but those who call a spade a spade, or refuse to tell the little white lies of social lubrication, invariably end up as warped and twisted individuals, unloved and unlovable. Not that I know anybody like that.

In sales, things are different. Selling is so full of sycophants, glad-handers, bootlickers, and asskissers that plain speakers are a rare and precious commodity. Outspokenness, if not quite next to godliness, is right up there with cleanliness and creative travel-expense claims. I know this for a fact because my kid sister used to work for a leading fashion retailer and won numerous salesperson-of-the-year awards. Her secret? Telling customers the truth. Yes, your bum does look big in that, madam. No, you're not a yellow polka-dot person, sir. Seriously, you should think twice about La Perla underwear, your lordship. They loved her for it.

Marvin Bower was renowned for plain speaking. The driving force behind McKinsey, a company often described as the Tiffany of management consultancy, Marvin took care of the "tiff" bit.[11] He was famous for telling it like it is. Whereas most management consultants, according to the ancient chestnut, borrow your watch to tell you the time, Bower borrowed your watch to tell you it's broken, and since you're the person who broke it, your time as CEO is up. None other than David Ogilvy once remarked that "If you send an engraved wedding invitation to Marvin Bower, the great man of McKinsey, he'll return it to you – with revisions!"

Plain speaking, as readers of my overwrought books will confirm, is not something I'm accustomed to. But even I have to acknowledge that Bower is the Freud, the Faraday, the

Henry Ford of failure. His entire career was built on failure. Or, to be more precise, on the causes of corporate failure and how best to avoid them. He was the quintessence of Fail Better, a power-packed, pint-sized Samuel Beckett.

Bower, in fact, was steeped in failure from a very early age. His father, a commercial real-estate specialist, would consult Marvin and his brother Bill on important family matters but often overrule their unworkable suggestions. At school, Marvin earned the ire of his prohibition-era teachers with a facetious newsletter called *Home Brew*. At college, according to his own testimony, he failed to make a full contribution to the life of Brown University, preferring to fraternize with the frat-set. While a student at Harvard Law School, he spent his summers as a law-firm intern collecting debts from clients who'd failed to cough up. Straight talking in such situations is an inestimable asset, I'm sure you'd agree. Marvin called it "dunning"; we call it "gentle persuasion"; others call it something else again. *Capisce*?

On graduating, our favourite enforcer was hired by a Cleveland law firm, Jones Day, which had its hands full with the disastrous corporate consequences of the Great Depression. Marvin spent three years studying defaulters, bankrupts, and calamitously collapsing companies at close hand. As Bower's biographer observes, "He typically began his study by interviewing the chief executive of the failed company, and then followed up by talking with any other staff members who might have insight into the causes of failure and the company's ability to recover from disaster."

From this in-depth investigation of eleven business tragedies, Bower concluded that the principal cause of failure was not lack of smarts on chief executives' part, but the fact that they were surrounded by browbeaten employees who wouldn't or couldn't tell their leaders the uncomfortable truth. Honesty may be the best policy, but it isn't exactly conducive to corporate preferment, much less rapid promotion.

Having learned the lessons of failure, and having realized that there was a place for impartial outside advisers, Bower had started to carve out his career path. Then fate took a hand. A position paper he'd written on a stricken clothing manufacturer fell into the hands of James O. McKinsey, founder of a Chicago-based "management engineering" firm who was working on secondment for Marshall Field's department store. In classic Chicago fashion, McKinsey made the Cleveland plain-dealer an offer he couldn't refuse, though Marvin's wife was worried, to put it mildly, about moving to the Windy City, stomping-ground of Al Capone and similar shady citizens. Two years passed before Bower took McKinsey's bait, and only then because Jones Day was cutting associates' salaries. Four years later, his new-found mentor died suddenly. Bower stepped into the breach, and along with three co-investors – two of whom were sexagenarians – he acquired the company and proceeded to build McKinsey into one of the most successful (and secretive) management consultancies in the world. It employed eighteen people when Bower took over. By the time of his retirement in 1992, 2,500 consultants were in harness. Today, McKinsey employs approximately 6,000 "associates," possesses 90 offices in 51 countries, has the ear of everyone who is anyone in business life and generates revenues of around $4.5 billion per annum. Not bad for watch repairers.

The best way to describe the firm that Bower built is as an unholy hybrid of McDonald's and the Medici. On the one hand, McKinsey is renowned for its Bower-implanted monomania. Just as McDonald's turned burger making into an exercise in invariant uniformity – mass-produced patties, identikit retail outlets, standardized service encounter scripts – so Bower built McKinsey into a consistently singular consultancy. The dress code, the *esprit de corps*, the "one firm" mentality, the selection process, the preferred analytical procedures, the infamous indoctrination (sorry, training) programmes, the look, layout, and style of the reports, the freakin' front doors of the offices worldwide ... all alike, all indistinguishable, all interchangeable. If not quite Stepford partners, they're definitely robo associates.

On the other hand, there's a fist. McKinsey is notorious not only for its (necessarily) brutally frank dealings with clients, but also for its ruthless "up or out" policy. This is an employee-winnowing process that sacrifices five out of six raw recruits. Interestingly, the rejects unfailingly retain undying affection for the firm that canned them. As lifelong members of a hyper-elite, semi-secret society of McKinsey cast-offs – there's even a for-alumni-eyes-only directory of the fallen – ex-associates are never short of a helping hand or fistful of consultancy contacts. Coupled with the company's "no comment" policy (a blanket refusal to discuss its practices or projects), this prompts the common accusation that McKinsey is akin to the Freemasons, religious cults, and, unsurprisingly given its unbreakable *omertà*, the Mafia. It's not called the Firm for nothing.

Most McKinseyites might concede the Medici comparison. It's been made so many times that denial is difficult. They might baulk, however, at the McDonald's parallel. A Michelin-starred McDonald's selling gourmet fare possibly – Arch Deluxe a speciality – but not the pattie-cake, pattie-cake burger-man scenario. Yet the Big Mac likeness is less ludicrous than it seems. Despite McDonald's much-repeated "have it your way" message, the burger company has always confined consumers to a fairly limited choice. It doesn't pamper customers, much less mollycoddle them. Marvin Bower was cut from similar cloth. He refused to call his customers customers. He refused to pander to his clients or tell them what they wanted to hear. His marketing strategy was predicated not on "push" but on "pull." That is to say, clients came to him; he didn't seek them out or make empty promises that he couldn't keep. In fact, he frequently turned down business when he didn't think a company would benefit from the solutions McKinsey sold. It wasn't so much "one size fits all" as "no fit, no sale." Howard

Hughes famously got the bum's rush from Bower, as did the US government on occasion.

This policy, it must be stressed, didn't mean that Marvin held his customers in low esteem or gave less than total commitment to tackling their problems. It meant that he refused to kowtow to customer demands or act on the assumption that the client knows best. The balance of power was crucial, as were the expectations brought to the table by both parties. "There is a psychological but real difference in attitude between the client who has asked for our help and the one who has been 'sold' and hence has a 'show me' attitude."

Needless to say, this no-nonsense, hire-us-if-you're-tough-enough sales strategy paid enormous dividends. Bower's blue-suited brigands became the toast of boardrooms worldwide. Far from being unwelcome, McKinsey was besieged by CEOs offering to lend their Omega timepieces. When Marvin's minions came to work for you, your company had finally arrived. The Fortune 500 fell like ninepins, as did every other ambitious organization that clamoured for the Firm's expensive services.

Of late, McKinsey has fallen into a degree of disrepute. Rumoured association with Enron's malefactors and alleged links to high-profile corporate failures including Sabena, Swissair, and GM, to say nothing of the Railtrack shambles and NHS debacle in the UK, have tainted the Firm's post-Bower reputation. Some say its famous facility for straight talking has segued into overweening arrogance. "We do not learn from clients," one associate is said to have said. "Their standards aren't high enough."

Tell us what you *really* think, Icarus.

RUPERT MURDOCH (1931–)
Toxic Sludge is Good for You

There are few less edifying sights than multi-billionaires bemoaning their lot. Avaricious CEOs lining their pockets while the workers go without is one of them, admittedly, but it doesn't compare with a whingeing billionaire who feels hard done by. And wants our sympathy to boot. What planet do these people live on?

In November 2006, the world was treated to the nauseating spectacle of Sir Richard Branson, super-rich plutocrat and serial cross-dresser, complaining at great length to anyone who'd listen. Big Bad Rupert Murdoch had beaten him to the punch. Branson's low-ball bid for troubled television network ITN had been trumped by Murdoch's News Corp., which swooped to scoop the 17 percent stake that all but blocked Branson's ambitions.

Richard was livid. Democracy is under threat. (Trembling lip.) The government should step in. (Catch in voice.) It's just ... it's just ... it's just *not fair*. (Is that a tear I see?)

Branson's we-wuz-robbed antics might have worked twenty years ago when British Airways was up to its dirty tricks. But after years and years of Virgin Trains, Virgin Cola, Virgin Radio, Virgin Atlantic, Virgin Media, and increasingly risible Virgin publicity stunts – his heart, clearly, is no longer in it – Sir Richard has lost much of the public sympathy he once enjoyed.[12] Many of those who witnessed his lachrymose exhibition, I imagine, would have seen a sore loser, a tosser throwing his toys out of the pram, a wanker in a woolly jumper, a corporate cry baby, a spoilt boardroom brat.

But, hey, that's just my opinion.

Unlike Branson, Rupert Murdoch has never enjoyed public sympathy. On the contrary, he is universally despised, distrusted, and disdained, not to mention dreaded by those who work for him. Variously described as the "Dirty Digger," "Rupert the Fear" and (in Fox TV's *The Simpsons*) "a billionaire tyrant," Murdoch is the bogeyman of UK medialand, Fox Television's Freddie Krueger, the Al Capone of Channel Ten.[13]

Al Capone, in fact, is a pretty fair comparison. Like Capone, Murdoch is blessed with considerable personal charm; he has an uncanny ability to pull the levers of political power; he makes his money by pandering to base human desires and doing things that some consider unsavoury; he is utterly ruthless when it comes to ridding himself of underperforming employees (legally, of course); and he has also been accused of incorrigible tax evasion. But not by me, Your Honour.

The only son of Sir Keith Murdoch, Australian newspaper owner and distinguished war correspondent, Keith Rupert Murdoch was born in Melbourne. He was educated at Geelong Grammar School, Australia's Eton, where he preferred playing truant at Flemington Racecourse to perfecting his Latin declensions. A gambler first, last, and always, Rupert was awarded a Rhodes Scholarship to Oxford University, where he famously sold advertising space in the student newspaper *Cherwell*. On his return down under he joined the family business, and despite his relative inexperience at the time of his father's sudden death in 1952, soon demonstrated his natural marketing flair and amazing deal-cutting acumen. A diet of populist sensationalism immediately increased the *Adelaide News*'s circulation – "Queen Eats a Rat" was a fairly typical headline – and by the early sixties Murdoch was spreading his corporate wings. He bought the *Sydney Daily Mirror* in 1960, acquired and discarded several other local papers, dabbled in radio, television, and recorded music, then established Australia's first national newspaper, a broadsheet, in 1964. *The Australian*, like many of his early ventures, almost came to grief. It lost money for years but gave Murdoch considerable cultural cachet and made him a political force to be reckoned with.

Britain was his next port of call. He acquired the unseemly *News of the World*, which was way past its best but had plenty of prurient potential. As it was a Sunday paper, its presses stood idle for most of the week, an indolence that a hard-driving, asset-sweating ass-kicker like Rupert couldn't indulge. He relaunched a daily, *The Sun*, and revolutionized British tabloid journalism with a judicious mix of trash talk, topless models, TV and team-sport coverage, tasteless *double entendres*, terrible pun-packed headlines, and agonizing alliteration-a-gogo prose. The ideal *Sun* story, it was said, contained three paragraphs. And every paragraph, three sentences. And every sentence, three words. And every word, one syllable.

The super soaraway *Sun* soon surpassed its principal rival, the *Daily Mirror*, and provided a platform for Rupert's US invasion. This commenced with the acquisition of underperforming regional newspapers in San Antonio and continued with the 1976 takeover of the *New York Post*. This did for the US mediascape what *The Sun* had done for the UK. For "Freddie Starr Ate My Hamster" read "Headless Body In Topless Bar."

The eighties were Murdoch's apogee of acquisitiveness. He scooped the *Sunday Times* and *The Times* in 1981, famously smashed the printworkers' unions at Wapping, swallowed Fox Studios in 1985, set up the Fox Television Network in 1986, and snaffled the bestselling US magazine *TV Guide* in 1988. After surviving a debt crisis in the early 1990s, Murdoch kept his megadeals a-comin', some successfully (BSkyB especially), some unsuccessfully (an attempt to buy Manchester United in 1999), and some somewhere in between (the satellite shenanigans in China). Today, News Corporation's empire stretches from shining sea to shining sea. All seven of them. Satellite television (Foxtel), sports franchises (Brisbane Broncos), movie studios (20th Century Fox), publishing conglomerates (HarperCollins), national newspapers (*Fiji Times*), glossy magazines (*Truck Australia*), radio stations (Nashe, Russia), advertising agencies (News Outdoor), record labels (Festival Mushroom), and social networking websites (MySpace) are just some of the many rich and fertile territories of the Murdoch archipelago.

News Corp., in short, is not dissimilar to Virgin – in overall scope if not specific sector – except that News Corp. is bigger, brasher, bolder, and better in almost every sphere, marketing included.

Rupert Murdoch is not renowned for his marketing prowess. His reputation as corporate raider, competitor crusher, political manipulator, and Genghis Khan of recruitment and retention is second to none, but customer coddling is not a skill most commentators associate with the Ozterminator. Yet Attila the Sun is a marketer of genius. From his earliest schooldays selling horse manure to old ladies in Melbourne to his *News of the World* heyday selling journalistic horse manure to the mouth-breathing masses, Murdoch has shown an uncanny ability to sell newspapers and media merchandise generally. His sales stratagems are as old as the hills: promotions, competitions, price cuts, sleazy scoops, sex-sells salaciousness, and, in the case of *The Sun*, carnival-barker-style TV advertising. He is not interested in worthy but dull journalism, that "newspaper of record" nonsense; he wants excitement, entertainment, energy, exposés, and ever-increasing circulation figures. Whether it be sudoku for eggheads, bingo for lowbrows, fantasy football for anoraks, or celebrity papshots for the starstruck, Murdoch is unmatched in his ability to move the merchandise. He expects to fail on occasion, as the Hitler diaries hoax and O. J. Simpson's *If I Did It* bear witness, but the mocking knocking headlines don't do him any lasting damage. Quite the opposite, if anything.

As his empire has grown, moreover, the Dirty Digger has made strategic use of cross-promotional possibilities. The *Sunday Times* reviews movies made by Fox, puffs books published by HarperCollins, and sings the praises of social networking websites like MySpace, while claiming that editorial decisions are unaffected by corporate considerations. If that's the case, how come the American characters in *Independence Day*, a big-budget Fox disaster movie, watch Sky News as they await their fiery fate?

The hard sell, then, is the essence of Murdoch marketing. Balls-to-the-wall price wars are his favourite selling tactic. Every brand he buys he moves resolutely downmarket because that's where the untapped opportunities are. His current preoccupation with China and India is motivated by the sheer number of what Ted Levitt terms "warm armpits." He has no time for happy-clappy, warm-and-fuzzy, hug-the-customers claptrap. He has no truck with artsy-fartsy business-school notions of total customer centricity. His principal customers, in fact, are the chief executives of News Corp.'s constituent companies, and without exception he treats them mean to keep them keen. Murdoch manages by fear, pure and simple. His lieutenants are subject to terrifying telephone calls in the still of the night. Apparently, these comprise either force 10 gales of fearsome obscenity or an eerie silence which the gibbering executives fill with gush, gabble, and your-wish-is-my-command genuflection. Such is his reputation that leading politicians crave Rupert's indulgence while abasing themselves before him. The Ozpontiff can make or break them, or so he implies, and the Aussie assassin expects regulatory favours in return.

In a world dominated by those who've swallowed the mainstream marketing ideology, Rupert Murdoch brilliantly bucks the simpering, servile, oleaginous, obsequious trend. Caring-sharing solicitousness is not part of the Murdoch package, nor is live and let live. Ask Richard Branson. "Freddie Krueger Ate My Houseboat." "Up Yours, Dentures." "Branson Pickled." "Gotcha!" "Headless CEO in Topless Brand."

AKIO MORITA (1921–99)
Do You Fail in Sony?

Most companies have their ups and downs, as Marks & Spencer's recent collapse and recovery bear witness, but few organizations have experienced the swings and roundabouts of fail-better fortune more fully or frequently than Sony. So predictable are the peaks and troughs of Sony's marketing trajectory – stupendous success followed by calamitous failure followed by even more stupendous success – that a branding equivalent of the Kondratiev wave can be posited. Let's call it the Sony Cycle. At least once a decade, the majestic domestic electronics icon experiences a seismic selling shift of Richter-scale proportions that rattles the windows and shakes the very foundations of the corporation. But each time it comes back stronger and more innovative than before.[14]

Take the company's first product, which almost ruined it. Founded by electrical engineers Masaru Ibuka and Akio Morita in 1946, Tokyo Tsushin Kogyo, as it then was, chose an electric rice cooker as its inaugural offering. Having rejected other product-market possibilities such as selling sweetened miso soup and building a mini golf course on a bombed-out tenement block, Ibuka and Morita settled on a rice cooker that switched itself off automatically when the contents were done to a turn. However, despite numerous attempts to allow for natural variations in rice quality and water quantity, the results were unfailingly underdone or overcooked.

Luckily, transistor radios provided a profitable alternative to temperamental cooking pots, though here too the spectre of failure loomed large. A tiny adjustment to the manufacturing process – replacing antimony with phosphorus – seemed like a good idea in the workshop but proved disastrous on the production line. Thousands of transistors were manufactured using phosphorous. Very few worked. It took seven months of experimentation, during which the company haemorrhaged capital, before the problem was cracked and the reject rate fell from 90 to 10 percent.

Having conquered the world with its wonderful transistor radios, and having developed a cute tape recorder after considerable trial and error, the renamed company's next landmark involved colour television. This was no ordinary leap, however. This was a Sony jump, a breathtaking bound to the edge of the electronic abyss. The unsurpassed colour of the Trinitron television, launched in 1968, was the happy outcome of seven years of frustrating failure as experiment after experiment with Chromatron technology – acquired from the US military in 1961 – produced nothing but blurred images, poor resolution, and queasy colour combinations. Despite desperate pleas from Sony distributors in urgent need of competitive products, Ibuka refused to copy or adapt existing technology, and almost destroyed the company as a consequence. Then, in a stroke of serendipitous inspiration, one of the 150-strong R&D team idly suggested replacing three conventional electron guns with a single gun that fired three beams. Trinitron never looked back and Sony's reputation as the Cadillac of electrical equipment was firmly established.

Only to be nearly destroyed a decade later by the Betamax debacle. Failure to mention Betamax in a book about failure is a dereliction of authorial duty, even though the story is familiar to one and all. Indeed, as a one-time owner of a Betamax, I can personally attest to the quality of the product, if not the aesthetics of the package. It was an ugly brute of a thing. I can also confirm that there were fewer movies available in the Betamax format than in VHS. Betamax's ignominious defeat at the hands of inferior technology was a lesson to all marketers everywhere, and a painful whack in the pocketbook for me personally. Needless to say, it was especially galling for Sony because the company once again bet the farm on a product, but unlike the Trinitron episode there was no upside other than the realization that software availability rather than technological sophistication determined the outcome of the VCR standards war.

The Betamax lesson nevertheless led to another Sony slip-up, again of catastrophic proportions. The search for suitable software suppliers sucked Sony into the tarpits of Tinseltown. Its acquisition of Columbia Pictures in 1989, at a vastly inflated price; its appointment of two flamboyant film-makers, Peter Guber and Jon Peters, to run the operation at vastly inflated salaries; and its profligate spending on movie production budgets, which bought market share at the expense of profit, all dragged the Godzilla of home electronics into the Hollywood mire. Four years later, Sony announced losses of $3.2 billion on its movie-making operation – one of the biggest losses in Japanese corporate history and one of the biggest beatings ever sustained by a foreign investor in an American company. The title of the (inevitable) book about the Sony shambles says it all: *Hit and Run – How Jon Peters and Peter Guber Took Sony for a Ride in Hollywood.*

Calamities like Columbia or Betamax or unworkable rice devices would've defeated most companies, as indeed would "minor" cock-ups like MiniDisc, Discman, DAT, Vaio desktops, or Sobax, a solid-state abacus. But Sony isn't most companies. It was founded by two titans, production whizz Masaru Ibuka and marketing maestro Akio Morita. Morita was brought up in the lap of luxury. The eldest son of a sake and miso manufacturer, he was groomed to take over the family business near Nagoya in central Japan. From an early age he participated in business decisions, attended board meetings and worked in every part of the factory, from bottle counting to soy-sauce tasting. The flavour of electronics was more appealing, however. He studied applied physics at Osaka Imperial University, turned his hand to wartime telecommunications research, and in 1944 was transferred to a task force developing a heat-seeking missile codenamed Marque. Ibuka was also a member of the task force and, despite drastic differences in social class, a life-long partnership formed between the two ambitious oddballs.

Morita's immersion in business stood Sony in good stead as the company struggled to find its feet. Family connections helped ensure the availability of venture capital and the all-important support of Japan's Ministry of International Trade and Industry. It was Morita's personal qualities, though, that set the company apart. Contra the Japanese corporate stereo-type – consensual, conservative, deliberate, low-profile – Akio was flamboyant, passionate, gregarious, outgoing, enthusias-tic, direct, and fun-loving. He moved to the United States in 1965 and spent most of his life there. His shaggy mane of silver hair with its dandyish centre parting made him instantly rec-ognizable. His networking abilities were equally remarkable. On friendly terms with every CEO worth knowing, he did much to foster Japanese–American relations and, an element of tokenism notwithstanding, effectively established himself as "the acceptable face of Japanese capitalism." By the mid-seven-ties, he was on the advisory boards of numerous blue-chip American corporations, from Pan Am to IBM.

Better yet, Morita exuded a kind of personal luminosity. His energy, effervescence, and enthusiasm shone out to all who came into contact with him. As a biographer notes, "Morita had the gift of incandescence. People observing him in action at various moments in his life were left with a similar impression that he 'lit up' a room with his presence."[15] Charisma may seem like a trivial personal trait, but as every salesman will attest, making the sale is as much about selling the seller as selling the product, service, idea, or course of action. Morita sold himself brilliantly and sold Sony simultaneously. Sony claims to be a company that sells dreams, visions, possibilities – its slogan for PlayStation was "Do you dream in Sony?" – and its leaders are required to *san-san to kagayaku*, shine dazzlingly like the sun.

Be that as it may, there's more to Morita's marketing ability than radiance. When it came to the nuts and bolts of brand development or tough-it-out negotiating tactics, Morita was a sunshine superman. During his first visit to the United States in 1958, Sony's tiny transistor radio met with rejection after rejection in the land of big is good, bigger is better, and biggest is best of all. The only exception was Bulova, a watch-maker, which negotiated a deal for 100,000 radios on the understanding that Sony's name would be replaced with Bulova's. Even though the company desperately needed the order, Morita refused to abandon his brand.

That said, Morita's marketing savvy didn't serve him well during the Betamax debacle, though he had grave doubts about the system and agreed to its release only reluctantly. His come-back with the Walkman, though, was one of the greatest back-with-a-bang moments in business history. The product was literally plucked out of thin air. It was worked up as a rough-and-ready plaything for Ibuka, something to keep him happy on long intercontinental flights. But as soon as Morita saw the prototype, he recognized its market potential.

Despite the opposition of almost everyone in the company, which was deep in the coils of compact disc development and the Betamax brouhaha, Morita made it happen without any pre-launch market research or painstaking R&D. This was unusual enough in itself, but he also insisted on a low price and lightweight earphones, even though a production run of 30,000 units would be needed to achieve economies of scale. When the salesforce said it was impossible to shift so many, he promised to resign as Sony chairman if all 30,000 failed to sell. He over-rode objections to the name – more "appropriate" alternatives were suggested for different markets – and demanded it be called Walkman throughout the world. He personally organ-ized the product launch, which again ran counter to Sony tra-dition. The gizmo was announced not in the company headquarters but in a public park, where members of the press were presented with cassettes containing prerecorded speeches and background music to be played on the new product while they watched Walkman-equipped rollerskaters, skateboarders, and cyclists cruise past enjoying themselves.

For a month, nothing happened. Then demand exploded. All 30,000 were sold within the next six weeks. Production couldn't keep up with demand. Capacity had to be doubled and trebled every month. The rest of the world followed Japan's lead. Walkman soon became one of those generic words like Hoover, Tupperware, Plasticine, and iPod that transcend their trademark and enter the language.

The prospect of failure wasn't something that bothered Akio Morita. Learning organizations, he believed, learned more from failure than success. Failure was never punished in Morita's Sony, even though the company stared into the abyss on several scary occasions.[16]

Sony's tribulations continue, as we noted in chapter 1. The Sony Cycle still turns. But don't bet against the Cadillac of electronics or the house that Morita built.

**AIMEE SEMPLE McPHERSON
(1890–1944)**

Canadian Comeback Kid

Death is always a smart move in the cultural industries. The untimely expiry of Cobain, Plath, Austen, Byron, Keats, Hendrix, Shelley, Monroe, Valentino, Lennon, Phoenix, Haring, Belushi, Basquiat, Buckley (*père et fils*), to name but a few, added immeasurably to their marketability.

The only thing better than death, career-wise, is resurrection. The dear departed then get to reap the rewards of their passing. Consider the recent digitally dependent comeback tours by Elvis Presley and Frank Sinatra, the latter supported by his still-living daughter. Consider the post-mortem appearances of Marilyn Monroe, Louis Armstrong, Humphrey Bogart, and James Stewart, all of whom make a good living doing television adverts. Consider Jesus Christ. Early death and rapid resurrection never did him any harm.

So successful is the now-you-see-me-now-you-don't-now-you-do-again manoeuvre that it forms an important part of the armoury of our Fail Incredibly Better marketers. Take Aimee Semple McPherson. Sadly forgotten today, Aimee was an extra-sexy evangelist, a superstar of the Roaring Twenties. A sort of holy Salome, she not only outshone most movie stars – at a time when the cinema was still considered improper – but toured the entire North American continent to massive crowds and mass hysteria. Then, at the absolute pinnacle of her career, when she had her own wildly successful radio station and a "temple" in Los Angeles that put Chartres cathedral to shame, she attempted a now-you-see-me publicity stunt that was so incredible it almost defies imagining.[17]

In May 1926, exhausted from her unstinting labours at the Angelus Temple, world headquarters of her International

Church of the Foursquare Gospel, Sister Aimee repaired to Venice Beach for the afternoon, where she treated herself to an invigorating swim in the Pacific. The charismatic evangelist never returned. Most assumed a horrible accident had befallen her. A major search and rescue operation was mounted. A volunteer diver died trying to find the lost soul; a frantic female follower committed suicide; another Good Samaritan plunged into the chilly surf only to suffer a heart attack that proved fatal. The nation was in mourning. The media were in meltdown. The lamentation was almost unbearable as tributes poured in, vigils were held, and uplifting hymns were sung by all and sundry.

Weeks passed. There was still no sign of the chosen one. Everyone – even her heartbroken mother Minnie – assumed Wonderful Aimee had gone to the great revivalist meeting in the sky. Then, praise the Lord and pass the collection plate, Sister Aimee reappeared. In a remote corner of Mexico, close to the American border. Hallelujah! Not only was she happily unharmed by her oceanic ordeal, but she'd abandoned her bathing costume for a *très chic* designer outfit, corset included. Ms McPherson claimed to have been kidnapped by three desperadoes called Steve, Jake, and – get this – Mexicali Rose. Fortunately, she'd managed to escape from their nefarious clutches and walked for thirteen hours across the fearsome Arizona desert to freedom. However, her unscuffed designer shoes showed no sign of a gruelling hike, and in any event high heels aren't exactly suitable for an exhausting tramp across rugged terrain.

Bedlam doesn't begin to describe the public's reaction, especially when an investigation was launched by LA's DA, Asa Keyes. There was no sign of the shack where Sister Aimee was held, nor of her alleged captors. It was rumoured she'd staged her disappearance as a cover for cosmetic surgery or possibly an abortion. There were suggestions she'd been spotted in the company of a portly slaphead with a wooden leg called Kenneth

Ormiston, who worked for her radio station and had also disappeared mysteriously. Recently divorced, he'd been seen with an attractive brunette en route to a love nest in Carmel. But Ormiston gallantly refused to name the lucky hottie.

When it became abundantly clear that the evangelist had been wasting police time, Asa Keyes assembled a grand jury and charged Sister Aimee with obstructing justice. In media terms, it was as if O. J. Simpson had shot Paris Hilton in Michael Jackson's Neverland while holding the King of Pop's pet monkey to ransom.

The nation was divided. Fellow hellfire-and-brimstone preachers claimed the pulchritudinous Pentecostalist had strayed from the straight and narrow and would burn for her tawdry transgressions. The faithful responded with a Fight the Devil Fund, which gathered the $250,000 necessary to defend Sister Aimee's honour in court.[18]

All the debate was for naught, though, because the LA DA suddenly – and conveniently – dropped the charges. As Asa Keyes was notoriously corrupt, a Bible-sized backhander was alleged. Not that Sister Aimee cared. Having overcome Old Nick's heinous henchpersons, she returned to her temple in triumph. If it hadn't exactly enhanced her reputation, the scandal had raised her profile even further. The donations from relieved supporters flowed in as never before. You couldn't make it up. It was all a long way from Salford, Ontario, where she started on her road to glory.

The daughter of an Irish immigrant, a widower who married his fifteen-year-old housekeeper at the grand old age of 50, Aimee Kennedy was brought up in a God-fearing family. Minnie, her mother, was a Salvation Army grunt who was washed in the blood of the Lamb and tougher than deep-frozen mutton. Following in her mother's matrimonial footsteps, adolescent Aimee fell for another Irish immigrant, lay preacher and part-time shop assistant Robert Semple. The preacher and his pregnant wife left for China as missionaries, but only Aimee and her daughter, Roberta Star, returned from their malaria-stricken mission to Macau.

A widow with child at nineteen, Aimee married an accountant from Rhode Island called McPherson and, understandably, soon abandoned domestic servitude for the life of an itinerant evangelist. A charismatic tent-preacher with the looks of an angel, she trekked up and down the east coast of North America from Labrador to Florida, saving souls, singing hymns, speaking in tongues, sermonizing like nobody's business, and, best of all, healing the halt, lame, blind, and deaf. Cripples were her speciality. "Pick up thy wheelchair and walk" was her miraculous exhortation, though this proved quite a burden for the newly ambulatory.

Brilliantly managed by Ma Kennedy – think Led Zeppelin's Peter Grant, only more menacing – the beautiful Bible-thumper drove her slogan-plastered Packard from town to town, slowly building up her flock. Thanks to Minnie's wonder-working power with the "paper contributions only" collection plate, Aimee gradually graduated from the tentpole circuit to concert halls, Pullman carriages, designer outfits, and the finest cosmetics that painted ladies could buy. The covetous Avon lady finally got the call from on high: get thee hence to La-La Land. After a perilous cross-country pilgrimage in the Packard, with Ma and daughter in tow, the sexy seraph arrived in the city of angels, where advance notice of her appearance attracted huge crowds. Word of mouth is hard to beat but word of God is beatific.

Within a few short years, Aimee had acquired sufficient shekels to build her temple, the roof of which glittered in the So-Cal sunshine thanks to its canopy of crushed seashells. A rotating cross perched on top; lit up at night, God's own logo could be seen for fifty miles. Sister Aimee also established a radio station, KFSG, whose transmissions were so powerful that they overflowed the assigned waveband and swamped competing stations. When censured by US commerce secretary

Herbert Hoover, the sainted evangelist replied "Please order your minions of Satan to leave my station alone. You cannot expect the Almighty to abide by your wavelength nonsense." Quite.

Whatever else she was, shameless Jezebel or celestial Esther, Aimee Semple McPherson was an out-and-out showperson. Her performances at the Angelus Temple – and long before that – were epic Ziegfeld-style productions involving actors, scripts, lights, costumes, heavenly choirs, golden trumpets ... the full ministerial monty, in fact. Charlie Chaplin advised on the staging and numerous movie stars attended to pick up tips from her "religious illustrations." Her message eschewed traditional burn-in-hell scenarios for an uplifting happily-ever-after prospect of heaven. Like Revlon's Charles Revson, Sister Aimee sold hope.

Selling indeed was central to the whole Four Square operation. A striking lighthouse-shaped logo, a widely circulated newsletter, a 400-strong network of branch churches known as the Salvation Navy, more media coverage than any celebrity might reasonably expect in the pre-*Hello!* era, and a dedicated radio station when radio was the medium of the moment were all part of the phenomenal McPherson package, as was a carefully calibrated programme of corporate social responsibility. Aimee welcomed the world-weary, housed the indigent, fed the hungry, healed the sick, and saved souls like there was no tomorrow. As a millenarian, indeed, she firmly believed that there was in fact no tomorrow, that the end was nigh or nearly nigh.

Then came the big swim. Sister Aimee recovered, of course. Her post-stunt ministry was more powerful than ever. She hired a full-time team of holy-roller telephone operators to provide succour for Four Square converts, who paid premium rates for the prayerful Pentecostal privilege. She worked like a Trojan to turn the Salvation Navy brand into the Fisherman's Friend of the God-fearing, good-living market segment.

Unwisely, though, Aimee remarried in 1931, an act she'd specifically outlawed in her preachments. The faithful soon lost faith. Even worse, she quarrelled with her minder/manager/ mother Minnie.

Things went to hell in a handbag thereafter. Aimee died in 1944 from a barbiturates overdose and was interred, appropriately, in the last resting place of the stars, Forest Lawn Cemetery. Just in case, a working telephone was installed in her casket. The foremost exponent of evangelical marketing knew full well what resurrection could do for a stage-managed brand revival.

ANDRÉ CITROËN (1878–1935)
Automarketer Extraordinaire

It is one of the quirks of the motor car industry, a sector whose
marketing expenditure is never less than lavish, that most of
its pioneers were averse to marketing. Many first-generation
carmakers came from a bicycle manufacturing or farm machin-
ery background, and as often as not were petrolheads at heart.
The car came first. The machine was all. Marketing was a necessary evil that had to be accommodated in order to move the
metal. But the metal was what really mattered.

André Citroën was a glorious exception to this rule.
Although trained as a mechanical engineer, Citroën chose not
to intervene in nitty-gritty design issues or to organize the
nuts and bolts of the manufacturing process. Nor did he get
involved in the death-defying road-racing antics of such rivals
as Ettore Bugatti and Enzo Ferrari. Citroën hired experts to
take care of design and manufacturing, and as for the exhibi-
tionist extravaganzas of daredevil drivers, he preferred to
avoid them, thanks all the same. If the Good Lord had wanted
André to drive, he wouldn't have invented chauffeurs.[19]

As a marketer of motor cars, nevertheless, Citroën was
unsurpassed. A latecomer to the automobile industry – his firm
was founded twenty years after Renault and Peugeot, let alone
long-forgotten marques like Panhard, Brasier, and Mors – he
quickly built Citroën into the biggest and best in Europe, a
position it retained until its dramatic collapse at the height of
the Great Depression. Although he was often described as the
Henry Ford of France, Citroën was the antithesis of the hard-
nosed, mean-spirited anti-Semite from Dearborn, Michigan.
Where Ford put the big into bigot, Citroën was a genial, jovial,
endearingly rotund individual who was blessed with the
common touch, chose negotiation over confrontation when

settling industrial disputes, and inspired a level of loyalty among workers – and customers – that was second to none. Like Sam Walton, Citroën understood that effective internal marketing formed the basis of effective external marketing.

As the offspring of an affluent Amsterdam diamond dealer who committed suicide when his son was only six, André wasn't brought up in the lap of unimaginable luxury. But he wasn't a penniless street urchin either. Expensively educated at the elite Ecole Polytechnique, he became a bit of a playboy, preferring to wine, dine, gamble, and dally with exotic dancers than earn an honest crust. However, things changed dramatically after the death of his mother in 1899. Devastated, he visited his married sister in Warsaw, where he stumbled upon a remarkable invention that changed the course of his life and ultimately furnished his company with its iconic logo, the celebrated double chevron. We're talking helical gears here.

Though much more efficient than standard straight-cut gears, helical gears were maddeningly difficult to manufacture. But Citroën know from his high-society contacts that modern American machine tools were up to the task, so he bought the Polish patent on the spot. Thus armed with international licensing rights, he took his helicals and ran. He established a gear-wheel manufacturing plant in Paris and spent the next few years building up his business-to-business business. A natural salesman, he successfully hawked his wares to factory owners in France and further afield. Even the *Titanic* came equipped with Citroën-built steering mechanisms. They worked perfectly; it was pilot error that was responsible for the great liner's iceberg encounter.

Having built up a successful business, André understandably enjoyed the fruits of his labours – gambling, partying, womanizing, Freemasonry, and so forth – until fate once again intervened. In 1908, one of his most important customers, the luxury carmaker Mors, was experiencing sales freefall. As a family friend, Citroën was hired to turn things around. He sprinkled his marketing magic dust on the stricken operation, and within five years sales increased tenfold. In fact, it was the Mors connection that prompted André's visit to the United States in 1912, where he visited Henry Ford's Model T factory at Highland Park and saw at once that the mass production, mass marketing approach could be adapted to European conditions. But his vision couldn't be implemented right away because war intervened. Using the skills he'd acquired while repositioning Mors, Citroën built a super-efficient armaments factory that achieved hitherto unheard-of feats of munitions manufacturing. It was a wonder of war-footing industrial production.

Come the armistice, Citroën was stuck with a state-of-the-art factory. So he turned to automobiles, establishing Société Anonyme Automobiles Citroën in 1919. By the time the production lines were up and running, it was the Roaring Twenties. Citroëns roared out of the gates. Above and beyond the propitious market conditions, André was blessed with two traits that catapulted his belated brand to the very forefront of a crowded field. First, he had an intuitive understanding of the needs of normal consumers. Unlike many of his rivals, Citroën wasn't an *eau de engine* kinda guy. He was never photographed posing in overalls or fiddling under a bonnet, much less participating in time trials.

Unlike his competitors, furthermore, he made his first car fully loaded. Most cars at the time were sold as a chassis plus engine and then fitted out by specialist coachbuilders. Buyers of Citroën's Type A, by contrast, got the complete package. Bodywork, bonnet, wheels, tyres, lights, horn, toolkit, driver's manual, and even electric self-starter came as standard. A snip at 7,250 francs, the car was not simply a lot cheaper than anything else on the market but extremely reliable to boot. It served as the springboard for a range of ever more sophisticated products: the Type B, C2, C3, C4, CV series, and ultimately the landmark Traction Avant, introduced in 1934.

Alongside the company's all-in products, Citroën rapidly established a nationwide network of franchised dealerships – 5,000 by 1925 in France alone – which sold and serviced the marque. Standard tariffs were imposed for service and repair work, and easy-fit factory-made spare parts were made available for the first time. André also offered a year's unconditional guarantee against all manufacturing defects, another first. Effective after-sales service, he shrewdly understood, was the secret of long-term customer relationships ("As soon as one sale ends," he once said, "another more important one begins").

Citroën was no slouch, moreover, when it came to converting waverers into purchasers, offering them low-cost hire purchase and car insurance schemes. He built up a massive card-index file of prospects – another benefit of the exclusive dealer network – and sent personalized mailshots to each and every one, complete with hand-written salutation and valediction. André Citroën was a relationship marketer before relationship marketing was invented.

The great man's second superlative talent was his prodigious promotional acumen. He advertised incessantly and with gusto. Numerous full-page ads in national and regional newspapers; countless thousands of posters; billboards beyond number; 150,000 road signs embellished with the company logo; double chevrons plastered on every available surface: hotel walls, private houses, farm buildings, bus stops. Bernayslike, he even set up a national bus service to increase consumer exposure to the ads at the stops. All manner of massively publicized endurance trials were mounted – trans-Sahara, trans-Africa, trans-Asia, trans-Antarctica – thereby demonstrating the cars' remarkable reliability and astonishing fuel economy. The company's praises were sung by an in-house orchestra. A monster flagship store, akin to contemporary NikeTowns, was built as a hommage to André's bedazzling brand.

Paris was brought to a standstill in 1924 when the opening

of the annual motor show was marked by an aerobatic display above the Eiffel Tower and a smoke trail that spelled out "Citroën" in kilometre-high letters. Between 1924 and 1934, the Eiffel Tower was illuminated from tip to toe at André's expense. Naturally, the light bulbs, all 250,000 of them, spelled out the sponsor's surname. Visible for 60 miles, it helped Lindberg navigate his way to the city of light at the climax of his landmark transatlantic flight.

Besides keeping his name in lights, Citroën kept his face in the gossip columns. A kind of jazz-age Richard Branson, he constantly popped up in 1920s newsreels, magazines, comic strips, and just about every medium of mass communication. This celebrity CEO consorted with the glitterati, hung out with Charlie Chaplin, and befriended painters, sculptors, and dancers, among them the peerless Josephine Baker, who famously claimed that she had two loves in her life: her country and her Citroën. André's gambling exploits were legendary too: he thought nothing of dropping stupendous sums during all-night sessions at Deauville casino. He tipped croupiers with cars. Surrounded by roiling rubberneckers while trying to play, he famously handed a 10,000 franc chip to an onlooker encroaching on his personal space ("Please be so kind as to take this and stop breathing down my neck"). Eating incognito in a restaurant, he once overheard a nearby diner extolling the virtues of Citroëns. On his way out, André handed the enthusiast a signed chit that entitled him to the car of his choice at the factory.

Such stories, of course, were widely circulated, more than repaying in free publicity what they cost in hard cash. Indeed, when charged with gambling away his company's assets, Citroën defended his easy-come, easy-go lifestyle with the words "If I were not a gambler, I would not be where I am today."

Be that as it may, Citroën's biggest gamble occurred in the early 1930s. At a time of sales travails and economic tribulation, he attempted to spend his way out of the Great Depression by introducing a vehicle that would be so far ahead of the pack everyone in Europe would want one. Viewed in retrospect, the Traction Avant established the template for the modern family car. Front-wheel drive, automatic transmission, hydraulic brakes, independent suspension, rack-and-pinion steering, ultra-frugal fuel consumption, monocoque chassis-less construction, and a stunning sweeping low-slung silhouette were all part of the Traction Avant package, as was a brand-new, up-to-the-minute manufacturing facility.

Unfortunately, the car was rushed into production and, having sunk every sou and then some into his quantum-leap model, Citroën arranged a knock-'em-dead demonstration for bankers, financiers, and desperately needed investors. The event was a disaster. The brakes locked, the gearbox failed, and the car broke down again and again. The company collapsed not long after, only to be acquired by Michelin and returned almost immediately to profit thanks to the Traction Avant wondercar.

By then, sadly, André Citroën was dead. Some said it was a broken heart. The doctors said it was stomach cancer. Whatever it was, the untimely demise of André Citroën marked the end of an automarketer extraordinaire.

SIR THOMAS LIPTON (1850–1931)
Makin' Bacon

Eminent Victorian grocer, marketer of the first order, and storyteller supreme, Sir Thomas Lipton was born in or around 1850, in or around a tenement building, in or around Glasgow. We don't know for certain, because he kept changing his story as his eminence grew.[20] What we do know is that Lipton's Ulster-born parents came from County Fermanagh farming stock, moving to Scotland for a better life during Ireland's post-famine economic depression. Frances Lipton and her husband, Thomas Lipton senior, opened a tiny grocer's stop in Glasgow and, supplied with fresh produce from the farm back in Fermanagh, managed to keep their heads above water. Just. Their youngest son, Thomas junior, helped out behind the counter, barrowed the Ulster butter and bacon from the nearby docks, and did whatever else he could to keep his ma 'n' da afloat. A handsome six-footer with personal charm to spare, Tommy proved a big hit with the ladies. Too big a hit, unfortunately, because an unspeakable incident of some kind occurred, though in decorous Victorian fashion, we don't know the details of young Tommy's amorous adventures.[21]

Suffice it to say that the teenager fled to the United States, where he wandered around doing odd jobs – tobacco picker, mule skinner, farm manager, door-to-door salesman – all of which duly featured in his quasi-fictional autobiography, *Leaves from the Lipton Logs*. Confabulation notwithstanding, Lipton's Stateside escapade ended with a prolonged period of employment in a New York department store owned by fellow Ulsterman, A. T. Stewart. Tommy worked in the palatial grocery department and picked up numerous tips about merchandise, display, pricing, and above all advertising, that were to prove invaluable back in Glasgow.

Bursting with business ideas, young Lipton returned home determined to transform his parents' grocery shop. But his father was adamant that expansion or a refit was out of the question. So Tommy went solo. He opened a small grocery outlet in Anderston, a densely populated working-class district close to the Glasgow docks. With its brightly painted fascia, imaginative window display, and low, low prices, Lipton's was an instant hit. Tommy intuitively understood – as did Sam Walton, Richard Sears, and similar pioneers of discount retailing – that low margin/high turnover operations were vastly superior to high margin/low turnover arrangements. Luckily for Lipton, most nineteenth-century grocers pursued the latter strategy.

Tommy cut prices to the bone on a strictly limited array of fast-moving goods: bacon, butter, and eggs, the staples of the Victorian working-class diet. Because of his narrow range, he could buy in bulk, negotiate extra discounts, and pass the savings on to customers. These unprecedented offers attracted additional customers, word got round, and a virtuous cycle of growth was set in motion. Before long Lipton opened a second Glasgow store, then a third. He secured his supply chain with a bacon-curing factory, spread his wings to surrounding towns – Dundee, Edinburgh, Aberdeen, Leeds, Liverpool, Belfast – and then established dedicated docks and loading quays in the butter-rich west of Ireland. The pace of expansion was unrelenting. All the profits were channelled back into the firm. All the savings were passed on to customers.

Before too long, Lipton was a byword for bacon. By 1898, he operated 4,500 retail stores and had distribution deals with more than 5,000 agents. Or so he claimed. The real figures were closer to 2,400 stores and 3,500 agents. What a card!

Actually, the Bacon King had a facility for porky pies. Hyperbole was his stock in trade. This was most fully expressed in his advertising campaigns, which were of unparalleled extent, extravagance, and exuberance. Lipton stamped his name on every conceivable advertising medium – handbills, billboards, newspapers, omnibuses, tramcars, factory chimneys, nautical buoys, hot-air balloons, and, believe it or not, the entrance to a tomb in the Great Pyramid at Giza. Its lintel was unforgivably incised with the ancient hieroglyph LIPTON.

Tommy's guerrilla-marketing attack on pharaonic Egypt was by no means his only innovation. Lipton's UK stores were advertisements in themselves, their window displays in particular being things of beauty. Or belly-laughs, at least. One of Lipton's earliest advertising antics was to commission cartoons by local artist Willie Lockhart. Typically depicting contented pigs on their way to Lipton's emporia, tearful pigs who'd lost their brothers and sisters in Lipton's, or contrasting queues of customers (grim 'n' gaunt on the way in, chubby 'n' cheerful on the way out), Lockhart's cartoons were a sales-generating sensation. People came from miles around to see the latest instalments, which were placed in the shop window every Monday morning. Complementing the cartoons were elaborate butter sculptures, creative displays of eggs, and illustrated price tags that were the talk of the town. "Have you been to Lipton's?" soon became a local catchphrase, or so Sir Thomas tells us.

Above and beyond the bedazzling window displays, Tommy Lipton was a master of marketing ceremonies. These commenced in July 1878 with a procession through the thronged streets of central Glasgow. It was led by three "Lipton's Orphans": enormous Ulster pigs dressed in brightly coloured outfits with advertising slogans on their flanks. A shillelagh-wielding stage Irishman drove the plump porkers through Glasgow's main thoroughfares, stopping traffic and creating havoc en route, especially when they "escaped." Such was the success of the pandemonium-inducing porcine promenade that Lipton repeated it with ever more exuberant additions for the remainder of his career.

Before long, the pigs were replaced with giant cheeses. We're talking colossal here: eleven feet high and two feet thick. The Brobdingnagian dairy products were paraded through the streets, placed in Lipton's shop windows, displayed for a week or two while the world stared agog, and finally dismembered by the great grocer himself on Christmas Eve to be sold off at an extra-low price per holiday slice. Not content with the massive crowds, Lipton gilded the elephantine lily with gold sovereigns that were salted throughout the stupendous Cheddars. Some lucky customers got more than they bargained for; others made do with the roller-coaster thrill of raised expectations and dashed hopes. Needless to say, the first cheese lottery in 1881 almost caused a riot, as did every Xmas rerun thereafter. The biggest cheeses on the planet had turned Lipton into one of the biggest cheeses in commercial life.

The publicity generated by the jumbo Cheddars was almost as enormous as the comestibles themselves. But not as great as the mastermind behind the PR campaign. Publicity, in point of fact, was Lipton's bread and butter. He sent free gifts to celebrity churchmen, soldiers, and aristocrats and got a wonderful promotional turn out of their innocent thank-you letters. He humbly proffered a giant cheese as his personal contribution to Queen Victoria's golden jubilee festivities and, after it was condescendingly spurned, promptly released the scornful royal reply to the rabid national newspapers. What a hoo-ha! He was prosecuted for one of his promotional flyers, a fake pound note that was so close to counterfeit it actually entered circulation and caused considerable monetary disruption in Scotland. Lipton got double mileage out of this promotional stunt: first when the note was issued to general hilarity, and second when he was prosecuted for his antisocial actions, again to widespread amusement.

Marvellous as the above exploits were, three other actions were integral to Lipton's marketing acumen. The first of these was attracting staff loyalty. Like Sam Walton, Sir Thomas garnered enormous grass-roots support from the shop-floor staff. Unlike Walton, however, he secured it through above-average wages, excellent working conditions, and employee benefits that were best in class. He also induced an incredible sense of organizational camaraderie through outings, picnics, sports days, and so forth, and paid particular attention to the training of staff at the customer-facing end of the operation, where the hard work was done and sales were made.

Second, he challenged for the America's Cup at a time when Anglo-American relations were awkward, verging on testy. Ridiculed for his lack of seafaring experience, our nauto-crat bought the best racing yacht money could buy, gave a heroic account of himself on several successive occasions and, as a self-made Irishman representing the Royal Ulster Yacht Club, received oceans of favourable publicity on both sides of the Atlantic. The fact that he failed to secure the trophy despite five glorious attempts only added to his fail-better allure.

The third factor was tea. Sir Thomas was noncommittal to start – reluctant, in fact – but when the enormous margins enjoyed by existing wholesalers and retailers became clear to him, he entered the tea business in a big way. He massively undercut the competition and, in an era when tea was becom-ing the British beverage of choice, his assault on the market provided the big-bejasus breakthrough that his butter- and bacon-based business needed. Cheap tea attracted the public in droves, not just to buy tea but to pick up other goods on impulse, and it infuriated the competition into the bargain. A war of words broke out, but rivals' outraged condemnation of Lipton's unconscionable actions served only to advertise the price-cutter still further. Tea also provided Lipton's entrée into the United States' beverage market and, benefiting from the America's Cup overspill, he milked it for all he was worth. At one stage, the sultry maiden on every packet of Lipton's tea – and the packaging was crucial – was as well known as Miche-lin's Bibendum or McDonald's Ronald are today.

Not any more, though. Lipton's tea is still sold as part of Unilever's brand array, but the golden days of giant cheeses, porcine parades, butter sculptures, and advertising on the Sphinx are long gone, as is the great grocerpreneur himself. Failure finally got the better of him.

GABRIELE D'ANNUNZIO
(1863–1938)
Eia! Eia! Eia! Alala!!

They say that truth is stranger than fiction. In Gabriele d'Annunzio's case it's necessary to specify which genre of fiction. Thriller comes closest, though it hardly does justice to the story of someone who was not only the greatest Italian poet since Dante but also the recipient of Italy's equivalent of the Victoria Cross, as well as a marketer more astute than Miuccia Prada, Giorgio Armani, Gianni Agnelli, Luciano Benetton, and Silvio Berlusconi put together.

So unbelievable indeed is d'Annunzio's life story that it has been embellished by innumerable fanciful imaginings.[22] Let's start with the facts. Despite rumours to the contrary – rumours, incidentally, that d'Annunzio propagated for their promotional value – the warrior poet was not born on the deck of a destroyer at the height of a storm at sea. He did not participate in cannibalistic rituals in Libya. He didn't compose an ode to his appendix during its extraction under local anaesthetic. He wasn't one of the conspirators behind the theft of the *Mona Lisa* in 1911. Nor was he assassinated by a Nazi spy on account of his outspoken opposition to the Hitler–Mussolini pact of 1937.

D'Annunzio, rather, was born in Pescara, a provincial city on the Adriatic coast in Abruzzo. His father was a fairly well-to-do dealer in wine and agricultural products, a pillar of the Pescara community. But he was also a dissolute womanizing spendthrift who saddled his family with enormous debts when he died in 1893. Gabriele eventually followed in his father's licentious footsteps – and then some – though at least he had the benefit of an expensive education at Cicognini College, a prestigious private school in Prato, Tuscany. It was there that he made his initial impact as a precocious teenage poet. With the aid of a subvention from his father, d'Annunzio published his debut book of verse, *Primo vere*, to considerable acclaim in 1879.[23] The young poet's upward trajectory continued with *Canto novo*, a collection of erotic odes, and a book of gruesome short stories, *Terra vergine*. Both sold well, as sex and violence tend to do. Similar volumes followed and were collected into a shock-horror anthology, *Novelle della Pescara*, in 1902. When the tome was published in English twenty years later, *The Times*'s reviewer concluded, not incorrectly, that they had been written by a madman.

After leaving school with several literary feathers already in his cap, d'Annunzio enrolled at Rome university. Conventional study wasn't for him, however, and he soon set out to conquer Italy's recently established capital city. He became a newspaper columnist, chronicling the comings and goings of Rome's glitterati. He wrote, at length and with considerable wit, of balls, parties, palaces, receptions, concerts, operas, literature, luxury lifestyles, bejewelled outfits, and the like. By 1883, he had the Eternal City's upper crust hanging on his every word, while everyone else talked about his pornographic love poems. Inevitably the "immorality" of *Intermezzo di rime* was attacked by imprudent prudes, boosting the book's popularity and enhancing Gabriele's growing reputation as an Abruzzese love machine.

Before long, our latter-day Don Giovanni was pulling off preposterous publicity stunts such as a staged squabble with his publisher over the "obscene" cover of *Il libro delle vergini*. D'Annunzio claimed to be shocked by the lurid images – three naked women cavorting with a garland of roses – and he wrote to the newspapers denouncing the cover for its "vulgar titillation." He also urged the public not to buy his shameful novella, while regretfully acknowledging that its contents did indeed include brothel scenes, sinful acts, and frolics of a seriously unseemly nature. It sold like hot pancakes on Shrove Tuesday.

D'Annunzio's reputation accelerated if anything in the 1890s as a consequence of his vast decadent novel *Il piacere*, his scandalous love affairs – the sordid details of which found their way into his books, thereby fuelling must-read-it rumours concerning the characters' real-life models – and his willingness to fight duels with literary rivals, infuriated cuckolds, and just about anyone who wanted a piece of him. A proponent of Nietzsche's concept of the *Übermensch*, he saw himself as a higher man and despised the common herd. What's more, when he lost his hair in a duel – I kid you not – the glistening slaphead promptly announced that baldness was a sign of a higher evolutionary stage. Modern man didn't need hair, he averred, because it no longer fulfilled a useful reproductive function. So he waxed his moustache and grew a natty goatee instead.

It is easy to dismiss d'Annunzio as a preening popinjay, much like his Irish contemporaries Oscar Wilde and W. B. Yeats. Nevertheless, he was a prodigiously gifted writer whose felicitous facility in every literary genre from short stories and epic poems to raunchy *romans à clef* and witty gossip columns is incontestable. So distinctive was his adjective- and adverb-laden style, and so idiosyncratic his personal appearance, that he became a prime target for *fin de siècle* satirists, cartoonists, humorists, affronted clerics, and the like. All good for the scribbling business, then as now.

By the early 1900s, d'Annunzio was world-famous. He lived in a mansion outside Florence that rivalled Trump Tower in its tastelessness, and lavished his impressive income on bibelots, collectables, knick-knacks, fast-acting pharmaceuticals, and faster-acting concubines. The rest he squandered. His affair with Eleonora Duse, the majestic Italian thespian who bent over backwards to promote his theatrical career, made them the Posh and Becks of *la belle époque*. Indeed, his semi-autobiographical novel based on their affair, *Il fuoco*, was a *succès de scandale* (and then some).

D'Annunzio successfully stood for parliament, though his

contribution amounted only to two speeches and yet another duel. His ambitious 1903 poem *Laus vitae* was hailed as a modern-day *Divine Comedy*, and his patriotic play *La nave* was received with rapture. Its nationalistic slogan "Arm the prow and sail toward the world" was seized upon and quickly entered the Italian vernacular. D'Annunzio was thereafter adopted by the Futurists, an avant-garde group of radical artists who embraced violence, militarism, and the machine. Filippo Marinetti, its spokesperson, maintained that Italy would be a future world power where the trains would run on time and bourgeois sensibilities would be abandoned for the enlightened leadership of dictatorial supermen such as Gabriele d'Annunzio, the wonderful warrior poet.

Filippo didn't have long to wait, in fact, before his warrior prediction came true. D'Annunzio was pretty much personally responsible for Italy's entry into the First World War. His spellbinding oratory swept all objections aside and overcame the elected government's wish to remain neutral. Commendably willing to walk the talk, d'Annunzio served with distinction in several branches of the armed services. He led torpedo-boat attacks in the Adriatic, survived hand-to-hand fighting in the front line, and flew numerous combat missions as a bona fide air ace. In fact, he famously flew over the Alps in a tiny biplane to drop self-penned propaganda leaflets on the capital of the Austro-Hungarian empire. He also kept the home fires burning with his patriotic poetry, which was read enthusiastically in the trenches though few infantrymen understood his luxuriant literary allusions. So influential was he that front-line dispatches from the general staff were often written in sub–d'Annunzio prose.

As if that weren't enough, our sublime self-publicist then staged perhaps the greatest publicity stunt of the twentieth century. Disillusioned by the Versailles treaty, which gave Italy no reward for its heroic effort on the Allies' behalf, d'Annunzio led an assault on Fiume, an Adriatic port whose ownership was disputed. Peremptorily claiming the territory for Italy even though the peace treaty awarded it to Yugoslavia, our shades-wearing war hero captured the city with the aid of 287 volunteers. For eighteen months he held out against the great powers despite a blockade, the hostility of the Italian government, and the fact that his legionnaires had to resort to high-seas piracy to keep Fiume afloat. Forget *Pirates of the Caribbean*, this was Pirates of the Mediterranean, with d'Annunzio as Sparrow. Eventually the warrior poet capitulated (on the toss of a coin!). But not before the Fiume episode had inspired all sorts of wannabe insurgents. The most noteworthy of these was a certain Benito Mussolini, who not only aped its uniforms and rituals – black shirts, death's-head insignia, raised right arm salute – but staged a copycat march on Rome in 1922.

In the aftermath of the Fiume fiasco, Gabriele retreated to a mansion on the shores of Lake Garda and spent the next eight years building a lavish Fascist-funded monument to his achievements. The Vittoriale degli Italiani boasts the biplane that buzzed Vienna, the motor launch that torpedoed the Austrian navy, the complete prow of a bleedin' battleship that juts out of a hillside one thousand feet above the lake, and countless mementos of his literary, military, and connubial achievements. It was declared a national monument in 1929, as indeed was d'Annunzio. Although his reputation suffered in the wake of the Second World War, he is increasingly seen as a Promethean poet, politician, philosopher, polymath, and, not least, a self-marketer of incomparable ability.

Like all great marketers, d'Annunzio was a utopian who painted compelling pictures of a perfect world where art and glory collide. Like all great admen, he had a flair for snappy soundbites, brilliant *bons mots* that captured the world's imagination in an unforgettable slogan. *Me no frego* (I don't give a fuck) was his most famous, but others included *Ognora desto* (Ever awake), *Semper adamas* (Always adamant), *Dant vulnera formam* (Wounds grant form), *Non nisi grandia canto* (I sing only great things), and *Eia, Eia, Eia, Alala* (his replacement for Hip, hip, hip, hurray).

Like all great marketers, what's more, d'Annunzio was chutzpah personified. The publicity stunts, the steamy novels, the Dantesque poems, the flagrant love affairs, the hair-raising duels, the war wounds, the tub-thumping speeches, the attack on Vienna, the shameless self-aggrandizement, and the insanity of the raid on Fiume all testify to this tendency. When stopped at gunpoint by the heavily armed Fiume garrison, d'Annunzio challenged the commander to make a choice: either surrender immediately or shoot the great Gabriele d'Annunzio in the heart. Our warrior poet then threw open his greatcoat to reveal a chestful of gleaming medals. Dazzled by the display, the commander ordered his troops to join d'Annunzio's legionnaires. Now that's what I call salesmanship.

ANNA HELD (1870–1918)
The Eyes Have It

Celebrity couples are ten a penny nowadays: Beyoncé and Jay-Z, Angelina Jolie and Brad Pitt, Catherine Zeta Jones and Michael Douglas, Paul McCartney and ... whoops ... should've gone to Nupsavers. Celebrity couples, what's more, have always been around: Charles and Diana, Bill and Hillary, Bogart and Bacall, Duse and d'Annunzio, Barbie and Ken, Adam and Eve, etc. etc. etc.

A hundred years ago, however, the *capo di* couples was Florenz Ziegfeld and Anna Held. They were by far the biggest stars on Broadway at a time when the Great White Way was at its whitest and hadn't lost its way. In our modern multimedia world, it's difficult to imagine a time before television, movies and the radio, let alone iTunes, YouTube, and Second Life. But this time last century, theatrical productions were the volcanoes of celebrity and Broadway was the Stromboli of fame.

Most of you will be familiar with Florenz Ziegfeld, possibly the greatest showman between the 1890s death of P. T. Barnum and Louis B. Meyer's reign of terror in 1930s Tinseltown. The spectacular *Ziegfeld Follies* – an annual confection of dazzling costumes, stunning stage sets, high-kicking chorus lines, and quick-fire vaudeville routines – is firmly fixed in the amber of cultural memory.

However, the real marketing genius when Broadway was the be-all and end-all and "Flo" allegedly ruled the roost was his all-but forgotten wife, Anna Held.[24] At the time, Anna Held was the superstar and Florenz Ziegfeld her hyperkinetic minder. At the time, Anna Held's name was on everyone's lips and newspapers didn't even take the trouble to spell her manager's surname properly, such was his perceived nonentity. At the time, Anna Held's 1910 separation from her philandering partner was considered Ziegfeld's ruin – if not quite his death knell, then certainly the loss of his main meal ticket. History has since been chauvinistically retrofitted to suggest that Ziegfeld was the real creative genius and the power behind the Anna Held throne. The reality is more complicated. Anna Held was the power behind the power behind the throne. The power bestride the throne, in fact. Anna Held was not a pretty puppet with Ziegfeld pulling the strings. She was an extremely astute businessperson and a marketing maestro in her own right.

Born in Warsaw, Poland, Anna was caught up in Czar Alexander III's pogroms of the early 1880s. Like many Eastern European Jews, she and her family fled to Paris, capital of culture, where her father opened a kosher restaurant. When it failed and the breadwinner fell ill with worry, his teenage daughter was forced into employment as a singing flowerseller. Little "orphan" Anna was talent-spotted by a prominent theatrical impresario, whereupon her coquettish qualities, pert provocativeness, and alluring eye-rolling quickly established her as a star of the burlesque circuit. The Folies Bergère, La Scala, and similar establishments in Holland, England, Germany, and Norway became her regular stomping grounds.

In Berlin, she seized upon a catchy little number, "*Die Kleine Schrecke*" ("Won't you come and play with me?"), and adopted it as her saucy signature tune. A naughty sing-along, it invariably brought the house down and provided Held's passport to prominence. By the mid-1890s, she'd become the embodiment of Parisian *oh la la*. She accentuated this image with savvy PR stunts, most notably her habit of riding horses astride rather than sidesaddle while wearing a scandalously short skirt, and doing likewise with bicycles when the cycling craze engulfed France in 1896.

A little bit of *quel horreur* never did the box office any harm. A lot of it worked wonders.

Then a hurricane hit. When tyro impresario Florenz Ziegfeld was encouraged to check out a charming soubrette in

London's Palace Theatre, he was a very minor player. His sole success in showbusiness was with Sandow the Strongman, a sideshow act at the Chicago Columbian World Exposition of 1893. Ziegfeld took the muscle-bound Adonis on tour, promoted his "fights to the death" with savage lions – heavily sedated savage lions, let it be said – and generally kept body-builder and soul together. When an opportunity arose to revive *A Parlour Match*, the long-running smash-hit farce, Ziegfeld was quick off the mark, and was actively scouting for European talent at the time of his chance encounter with Anna. Novice producer he might have been, but he knew star quality when he saw it.

Despite Anna's misgivings, he talked her into taking the transatlantic steamer to America. The two of them arrived in New York in August 1896. Meantime the press had been primed with fanciful stories about the "French" coquette. Posters with the slogan "Go to Held" were plastered all over the city. Her pulchritudinous picture appeared in *The Police Gazette*, a gilded-age equivalent of *FHM*, *Maxim*, or *Nuts*. She was greeted on arrival by a party of theatrical luminaries including Lillian Russell, whose position at the summit of American cheesecake she would shortly usurp. And she gave her first press conference in the kind of flimsy negligée that we today would call an overcoat. With a charmingly inadequate grasp of English, she assured the slavering newshounds that her hobbies were visiting the poor and paying their rent, while vociferously denying that her show was in any way rude or shocking. The kind of denial, in short, that attracts sensation-seekers and moral guardians alike.

The latter, needless to say, blew a collective gasket when the foxy lady shimmied onstage in *A Parlour Match* and seductively cooed her signature showstopper, "Won't you come and play with me?" Words like wanton, brazen, bawdy, and worse peppered the reviews and a must-see show was on its way. Before long, Anna's resplendent features appeared in countless photospreads, as well as on the packaging of cosmetics, hair tonic, sheet music, silver polish, corsets, bicycles, footwear, gloves, scarves, muffs and – oo-er, missus – foundation garments. Anna Held was a brand a hundred years before the Sugababes or the Spice Girls. Her endorsements even stretched to cigars, which is more than Brand Bill Clinton ever managed.

A Parlour Match was little more than a cameo appearance, albeit one that showcased her talents to perfection. However, if the girl with the beckoning eyes was to stay in the public eye, she needed something more substantial. After touring *A Parlour Match* around the country to popular acclaim, provincial outrage and standing-room-only box office, Anna girded her much-lambasted loins for the next theatrical challenge. Unfortunately, as its title suggests, *La Poupée* demanded a puppet-like performance that didn't take advantage of the saucy soubrette's idiosyncratic expressiveness. It flopped, as did Ziegfeld's next attempted showcase, *The French Maid*. Bizarrely, Anna wasn't cast as the eponymous lead. She came on for only a short turn in the second act, much to the expectant audience's chagrin. The critics caned her mercilessly, so to speak. One churlishly concluded "She can't sing, she can't dance, she doesn't even have a good figure." He also recommended that the theatre be fumigated to remove the stench of moral turpitude.

The stink continued with the chanteuse's next vehicle, *By the Sad Sea Waves*. It too sank without trace. Ziegfeld clearly didn't understand the Anna brand promise. Understandably, the artiste took matters into her own hands and, with the assistance of ace Broadway playwright Harry B. Smith, developed an American version of the French play *La Femme à Papa*. With Anna in the starring role, *Papa's Wife* opened in November 1899 to massive acclaim and monstrous box office. It was the sensation of the season, and several seasons thereafter. It featured Anna's full stagecraft repertoire, including a brilliant tipsy scene in the second act. It also included a series of breathtaking costume changes, an Anna-innovation that Ziegfeld was to exploit thereafter. The critics raved. The audiences went ape. The ticket touts made a fortune. The press went wild for Anna-items, as did sponsors, advertisers, and just about anyone with anything to sell. The dazzling costumes in particular opened up an entire new market, establishing Held as a fashion plate. Her subsequent stage shows always featured the latest fashions from Paris. American fashionistas flocked to see the designs and take notes on them for home reproduction on Isaac Singer's marvellous contraption, the sewing machine. Held was not only a singing, dancing sensation, she was a supermodel to boot. With an eighteen-inch waist and wondrous hourglass figure, Anna Held was Kate Moss, Heidi Klum, Gisele Bündchen, Christina Aguilera, Nelly Furtado, and Britney Spears combined. *Whoops*-era Britney, that is.

The hits came thick and fast after *Papa's Wife*. *The Little Duchess* eclipsed *Papa*'s dazzling success and *The Paris Model* went stratospheric. It couldn't last, of course. Sick and tired of his serial infidelities, Held finally divorced Ziegfeld in the aftermath of their last great collaboration – and single biggest hit – *Miss Innocence*. Flo went on to new theatrical successes with the *Follies* in particular, as well as a string of stupendous hits (*Show Boat*, *Whoopie*, *Rio Rita*) and woeful misses (*Simple Simon*, *Hot Cha*, *Betsy*). Anna had triumphs of her own, such as *Follow Me*, the movie *Madame La Présidente* and, backed by her own production company, *Anna Held's All-Star Variety Jubilee*. She also reinvented herself as a battlefield angel. She served gallantly on the Western Front as a nurse-cum-entertainer-cum-morale-raiser-cum-national-icon. Sadly, she contracted myeloma at the peak of her war-hero popularity and died aged 48 in 1918.

A hundred years on from the saucy chanteuse's zenith, Florenz Ziegfeld is regarded as the great marketing impresario of his era. He was a promotional genius, no question. His early

PR stunts for the pert protégée – the kissing contests, the car races, the jewellery heists, the headline-grabbing claim that Anna bathed in fresh cows' milk – were works of marketing art in themselves. However, it's important to appreciate that the *Follies* were Anna Held's idea, the dazzling costumes were Anna Held's idea, the emphasis on glamorous chorus girls was Anna Held's idea, the show that really launched her, *Papa's Wife*, was Anna Held's idea, and the song that attracted so much attention, "Won't you come and play with me?" was Anna Held's pre-Ziegfeld signature tune.

The business brains behind the partnership belonged to Anna Held. She was the one who "retired" in 1911 with a million dollars safely banked; she was the one who managed the Anna Held brand so brilliantly; she was the star at a time when Ziegfeld was the backroom bagman. Anna learned a lot from Ziegfeld, but he learned much, much more from the girl with the champagne eyes.

DALE CARNEGIE (1888–1955)
So Not How To

If ever anyone shouldn't have become a business behemoth, it was surely Dale *How to Win Friends* Carnegie. A singularly unprepossessing individual – snaggle-toothed, tongue-tied, big-eared, short-sighted, with appalling interpersonal skills and a Midwestern accent as thick as molasses – he turned himself into the guru of getting on, the very model of a modern marketing manager. Almost by accident, it has to be said, though not *entirely* by accident.

Dale Carnagey, as he was originally called, may have had many nicknames bestowed on him by the good farming folks of Warrensburg, Missouri, but "Lucky" wasn't one of them. The only person who was unluckier than Dale was his dad, who failed as a hog breeder, worked an arable farm prone to flooding at harvest time, and on one heart-rending occasion bought an expensive jackass that died the day it was brought home from market.[25]

Sensibly deciding not to follow in his father's foolhardy footsteps, Dale set out to be a teacher. He scraped into State College, where he was profoundly embarrassed by his parents' poverty, by his pig-farming background, by his gawky, big-eared appearance, by his shabby, ill-fitting clothes and by the fact that, unlike the rest of the students, he couldn't afford to live on campus. So he rode in to college on a broken-winded mare, then returned to the farm each evening and slopped out the pigs. A social outcast who contemplated suicide on several occasions, he once plucked up the courage to ask an attractive student out on a date. She laughed in his face.

Despite or possibly because of such slights, Dale decided to make a name for himself on campus. Sporting achievement, the usual route to collegiate eminence, was a non-starter.

However, public speaking was regarded as an acceptable alternative. Unfortunately, he wasn't very good at it. He entered a dozen contests and lost them all. But he kept plugging away, memorizing Abe Lincoln speeches as he rode to and from college. After a solid year of abject failure, our farmboy struck gold with the Gettysburg Address. Dale was on a roll. Until he hit a rock. Lacking Latin, he failed to graduate from Warrensburg. A teaching career was out of the question.

Sales seemed like a reasonable alternative, especially for someone with (by now) considerable oratorical abilities. He'd talk his way to success. Except that he didn't. International Correspondence School courses were a hard sell, especially in the hard-scrabble heartland of western Nebraska. Dale failed and failed again. The only sale Carnagey closed was with a telegraph linesman, who was stuck up a pole at the time. With his escape route blocked, the sap found himself talked into taking a correspondence course in electrical engineering.

Defeated by all but the linesman, Dale decided to return to the meat business. Purely by chance, he arrived in Omaha at a time when meat packing giant Armour and Co. was hiring sales reps. He was assigned to a remote part of South Dakota, where he did fairly well thanks largely to his dogged refusal to take no for an answer, which extended even to accepting payments in kind rather than cash. Eventually he was offered a management position at potted-meat HQ, but he had bigger fish to fry. He was going to be an actor. A star. On Broadway. In 1910, when the Great White Way was white hot and going Held for leather.

Nothing if not ambitious, Carnagey the would-be thespian took a one-year course at AADA (American Academy of Dramatic Arts). On graduation, he landed the first part he auditioned for. An illustrious theatrical career beckoned. But not for long. The touring review he joined, *Polly of the Circus*, wasn't exactly the greatest show on earth. When it ended, Dale couldn't get another part, so he went back to being a salesman.

A motor-car salesman this time. Regrettably, his previous experience with potted-meat products didn't stand him in particularly good stead, especially as Packards were the Porsches of their day and Manhattanites were notoriously demanding customers.

Ere long, he packed Packard in and set out to do what all congenital failures do: write a bestseller. To keep the wolf from the door while he wrote the Great American Novel, Dale applied for a part-time teaching position at Columbia University, then as now an imperious Ivy League institution. Lacking a college degree and encumbered by a thick hick accent, he wasn't exactly welcomed with open arms. New York University passed on the yokel as well. Dale wound up in Harlem at the YMCA, teaching evening courses in public speaking. So underwhelmed was the Y's director that he refused to pay the standard salary of $2 per class. Instead, he put Carnagey on commission, fully expecting Boondocks Boy to bomb out.

But he didn't. Carnagey had found his niche. Before long, his public-speaking course was generating $30 a night in commissions. Getting ahead was the watchword of the Progressive Era and, with wave after wave of immigrants passing through Ellis Island, Dale was on the proverbial pig's back. Granted, he wasn't as happy as the equally proverbial pig in shit. He lusted after literary acclaim. Literary acclaim didn't reciprocate. His Great American Novel, *The Blizzard*, was so abysmal that even his agent begged for mercy. He wrote a couple of non-fiction works. They didn't sell. He tried to repeat the theatrical triumph that was *Polly of the Circus*. Sadly, the show went dark after a week. The only thing he was good at was teaching public speaking.

He did, however, have the smarts to change his name to Carnegie in 1916, claiming to be distantly related to the celebrity steel magnate Andrew Carnegie. To help cement the alleged link, he opened a course administration office in Carnegie Hall.

For the next twenty years or thereabouts, Dale Carnegie earned his corn on the self-help adult education circuit. Substantial sheaves of it. His enthusiasm was not just infectious but the single most important lesson he taught. Be enthusiastic. Be effervescent. Be energetic. Be eager. Believe. Truly believe. Believe in yourself and good things will happen. They even happened for him, believe it or not, as accident once again played an important part in the former farm boy's progress.

In the early 1930s, one of Carnegie's students was so enthused by the great enthusiast's exhortations that he invited a neighbour along on a whim. That neighbour was Leon Shimkin, an editor at Simon & Schuster. Equally enthused by the effervescent enthusiast, Shimkin felt there was a book in Carnegie's self-help course. But Dale didn't want to know. Simon & Schuster was one of the publishers that had rejected his first two manuscripts and our failed novelist still bore the scars. Shimkin persisted. Carnegie said no. Shimkin hired a stenographer who transcribed one of Dale's lectures. When the reluctant guru read the transcript, he was pleasantly surprised by his own words and agreed to pick up his pen once more, despite numerous prior failings.

But writing still wasn't his forte and he took two whole years to hack out a draft. Rambling, repetitive, and contradictory, the manuscript was put into production. Reluctantly, it has to be said. Hopes weren't high. A tiny print run of 1,200 copies was ordered. Shimkin had a great promotional idea up his sleeve, however. Simon & Schuster agreed to send free copies of *How to Win Friends and Influence People* to 500 graduates of the Dale Carnegie course, with an accompanying letter urging them to pass the book on to others who might benefit from its wisdom. Shimkin's stunt brought orders for 5,000 copies. Word of mouth turned into a roar, Simon & Schuster splashed out on a full-page ad in the *New York Times* (which cunningly included a quotation – not an endorsement, a *quotation* – from Andrew Carnegie), and by the end of 1936, *How to*

Win Friends and Influence People had firmly established itself at the top of the bestseller list.

Carnegie's career took off on the back of the book he was unwilling to write. He appeared on radio, delivered prestigious lectures, wrote syndicated newspaper columns, franchised his self-help educational system, and, in the depths of the Great Depression when encouraging recovery was high on the national agenda, he established himself as America's foremost how-to guru. The critics, needless to say, pounced on his platitudinous "smile, smile, smile" philosophy. He was butchered like the hogs he once tended. Parodies soon appeared, most notably Irving Tressler's *How to Lose Friends and Alienate People*, which included such chapters as "How to Make a Poor First Impression," "How to Discourage Overnight Guests," and "Always Turn a Conversation into an Argument."

As ever, however, the diatribes of East Coast intellectuals only added to Carnegie's allure. The fact that Dale failed to adhere to his own precepts didn't halt the how-to steamroller either. Off stage, the great enthusiast was shy, standoffish, and frankly unenthusiastic. His interpersonal skills were lamentable. He was often argumentative, something he advised against in his bestseller. He tried to memorize his speeches, even though he discouraged the practice in *How to*. For a man who preached the gospel of personal magnetism, Dale Carnegie was decidedly uncharismatic. For someone who knew the secret of making friends, he had very few to speak of. Even his wives couldn't stand him.

All the same, it's hard to argue with success. Carnegie's operation is still going strong. Self-belief makes the world go round. Clichés cut a long story short. Aphorisms hit the nail on the head. You mark my words.

ANTON MESMER (1734–1815)
Sleepy, Sleepy, You Are Feeling Sleepy

Marketing, it pains me to admit, is the haunt of a charlatan or several. Most agree that the pre-eminent scamp of modern times was James L. Vicary, the mastermind behind subliminal advertising. At the height of the 1950s' fad for motivation research, he claimed to have conducted rigorous experiments into the power of advertiser-implanted suggestion. Two cinema audiences were exposed to movies containing subliminal embeds: messages that couldn't be detected by the naked eye, specifically "Drink Coke" and "Eat popcorn." Sales of Coke and popcorn soared among the cinemagoers, thereby proving that advertisers could mess with the minds of consumers and get them to buy through autosuggestion. Official outrage was unbounded and to this day subliminal advertising is banned in many western nations.[26]

Suffice it to say, Vicary's experiments never took place. They were a publicity stunt designed to establish his reputation as America's motivation researcher of choice. The official outrage was a consequence of Cold War paranoia about brainwashing. Many senators believed that just as Reds were under their beds, Commies were up to no good in the nation's pantries. Khrushchev, the cunning Russian devil, had opened a second front on the Kitchen Debate with Nixon.

The sad reality is that subliminal adverts don't work, though it's not for want of trying. For years I've been salting my writings with the insidious embeds "Buy Brown's books" and "Read Brown's latest," but I'm still waiting for that megabestseller. Unless, of course, readers inferred that the embeds referred to Dan Brown. Damn and blast ...

Whether subliminals work or not, James L. Vicary was a rank amateur compared to the real marketing genius behind consumer autosuggestion. Aptly described as the "wizard from Vienna," Franz Anton Mesmer was a highly respected member of bourgeois society. He was a fully qualified doctor. He had a successful upmarket practice. He married into money. He was a patron of the avant-garde arts, Wolfgang Amadeus Mozart in particular. Until fate intervened.

A friend of the family, Francisca Oesterlin, suffered from a particularly debilitating form of nervous prostration that no amount of bleeding, purging, or blistering would alleviate. Observing the ebb and flow of her attacks, Mesmer maintained that she was afflicted by an imbalance in "animal magnetism," an undetectable fluid, akin to gravitation, that suffused the entire cosmos and all its component parts, be they animal, vegetable, or mineral. Yeah, I know, I know, but it seemed like a good idea at the time.[27]

Magnets, fortunately, provided a means of channelling the universal fluid, and by passing a couple of the suckers over Ms Oesterlin, Mesmer was able to manoeuvre the "tides" in her nervous system, induce a relaxed trance-like state, stimulate violent cathartic convulsions, and thereby effect a lasting cure. Don't try this at home.

Anton, I grant you, wasn't the first to recognize the therapeutic value of stroking. A particularly important precursor was Valentine Greatrakes, an Irish faith healer who cured by the laying on of hands. But Mesmer was the first to offer a formal theoretical explanation, the first to put the phenomenon on a scientific basis, and the first to seek the approval of the medical establishment of which he was a respected member.[28] The last of these was regrettably not forthcoming – despite Mesmer's long line of satisfied customers – because invisible universal fluids were considered much too close to quackery for comfort. As the procedure also involved suspiciously intimate contact between (male) doctor and (female) patient, it was morally questionable as well. Indeed, when one nubile patient, Maria Theresa Paradies, refused to leave Mesmer's care and return to her parents as instructed, the ensuing scandal forced the Herr Doktor to high-tail it out of Vienna.

By the time our defrocked physician reached Paris, his animal magnetism roadshow had added an all-important element of pizzazz. The magnets were abandoned for a mesmerizing stare, elaborate hand-waving exercises, and a singularly striking pose that can only be described as akin to a chronic constipation sufferer caught in the moment of realization that Ex-Lax works. Happily untroubled by low self-esteem, furthermore, the perfumed, periwigged, purple-clad peacock took the city by storm.

Such was the popularity of his therapeutic salon – an eighteenth-century combination of the Betty Ford Clinic, Walt Disney World and the Four Seasons Hotel – that Mesmer was forced to develop a system of mass therapy, a kind of proto-production line. This consisted of several *baquets*: enclosed wooden boxes filled with "magnetized" water whose healing power was transmitted by protruding metal rods that were placed against the patient's afflicted parts. The unfortunates without access to the therapeutic rods were roped together like mountaineers on the Matterhorn. Padded crisis rooms were set up for those unable to control their convulsions. Musical accompaniment was provided by pianoforte and the glass harmonica, a contraption consisting of half-filled bowls of water which emitted musical notes when struck. Our constantly circulating consultant-in-chief armed himself with a healing wand that pole-axed passing patients when pointed in their general direction. And several handsome pre-operatives prepared the mainly female clientele by staring meaningfully into their eyes and gently stroking their ... well, you get the picture.

What's more, as a nothing if not public-spirited citizen, Mesmer magnetized nearby trees so that the indigent could grab one of many dangling ropes and get their magnetic influx for free, albeit al fresco. Indeed, one enraptured aficionado of the great man's system suggested that the headwaters of the river Seine be magnetized at source, thereby ensuring that the entire Pays de France benefited from the therapist's monumental medical breakthrough.

Not content with staggering financial success and enormous popular acclaim, the charismatic physician and proud possessor of the original magnetic personality still hankered to have his system endorsed by the scientific establishment. After extensive political manoeuvring by a well-connected protégé called Alain Delson, a royal commission was set up in 1789 and charged with investigating the animal magnetism outbreak. This twelve-man task force was headed by Benjamin Franklin, then US ambassador to France, and included such other luminaries as Joseph-Ignace Guillotin and Antoine-Laurent de Lavoisier (the latter had an unfortunate brush with the former's famous mechanism five years later). Empiricists, rationalists, and sceptics to a man, the commission allowed themselves to be mesmerized (unsuccessfully), spent long hours roped together at a *baquet* (without so much as a twitch, let alone a convulsion), and conducted various experiments on patients known to be particularly strong conductors of animal magnetism (they fell into trances when misinformed that a mesmerist was present and failed to respond when an exponent was behind a paper screen). The commission concluded that while healing unquestionably occurred, it was due not to animal magnetism but to the imagination of the patients.

Mesmer may have failed the formal medical test, but his humiliation was a solid-gold marketing triumph. As with Vicary's subliminals, official condemnation did more to encourage than eradicate his animal magnetism. When the chastened therapist threatened to leave town and take his system with him, a barely controlled panic broke out among his predominantly aristocratic clientele. Marie Antoinette herself was forced to intervene.

So popular indeed had Mesmer's methods become that Anton established a training college and franchised his therapeutic system. Before long, all sorts of mesmerist societies emerged. Innumerable practitioners of the ignoble art (or variants thereof) crawled out of the nineteenth-century woodwork. Particularly noteworthy were Elisha Perkins from Plainsfield, Connecticut, who patented metallic tractors and tackled every disease known to man or beast until yellow fever proved too much for him in 1799; John Elliottson, who promoted mesmerism in England by means of a dedicated periodical, *The Zoist*, only to be forced out of his professorship at University College Hospital; and Jean-Martin Charcot, who specialized in the treatment of hysteria, that peculiarly Victorian condition, and had a student, Sigmund Freud, who went on to greater things. Then there was the incomparable James Esailade, who mesmerized elephantiasis sufferers in imperial India and then operated on their unanaesthetized scrota. Ouch!

More prosaically, the mania for animal magnetism spawned all sorts of pseudo-medical paraphernalia such as Wilsonia Magnetic Garments, Richardson's Magneto-Galvanic Battery, the Edson Electro-Magnetic Garter, Dr Scott's Electric Corset, and, as late as the 1930s, Gaylord Wilshire's I-ON-A-CO, a kind of magnetic plug-in dog collar. In recent years, magneto-electro therapies of one kind or another have made a comeback. Maggie Thatcher was partial to periodic immersion in electric baths, which explains a lot. Animal magnetism is no less popular among the management community. The consultancy circuit is chocka with hucksters hustling animal-based metaphors that purport to do wonders for afflicted organizations – purple cows, dancing elephants, corporate squirrels, big fish eaters and, for all I know, haemorrhoidal hippopotami.

Contemporary animal magnetism works, moreover. How do I know? James L. Vicary told me. Mind you, I was mesmerized at the time ...

JEFF KOONS (1955–)
Art with a Capital M

There's only one thing worse, the sainted Oscar Wilde adroitly observed, than being talked about, and that is – all together now – not being talked about. An astute self-marketer, Oscar knew what he was talking about, though in today's world of Facebook, MySpace, Bebo, FriendsReunited, and similar social networking websites, it sometimes seems that no one is not being talked about. Not not being talked about is the norm nowadays.

When it comes to not not being talked about, Jeff Koons is close to the top of the chat chart. Few contemporary artists have divided opinion more than kitschy, kitschy Koons. Robert Hughes, the irascible Australian art critic, considers him a "starry-eyed opportunist *par excellence*" who produces "nauseating ... unctuous ... enervated claptrap." Michael Kimmelman thinks he's "artificial," "cheap," "cynical," an egregious exponent of "self-promoting hype and sensationalism." Mark Stevens deems him a "decadent artist who serves the tacky rich." Others are even less enthusiastic.[29]

Jeff Koons may or may not be the embodiment of another Oscar Wilde aphorism, "All art is quite useless" – he's the best thing that ever happened to bad taste – but everyone agrees that the kitschmeister's a marketer of the first magnitude. His most quoted line is "So much of the world is advertising, and because of that, individuals feel they have to present themselves as a package." Jeff practises what he preaches about packaging. One of his best-known paintings, *Pink Bow*, is of a giant package covered in shiny wrapping paper. Easter eggs, Valentine hearts, funfair rides, ice-cream sundaes, Mickey Mouse-alikes – the appurtenances of holiday celebrations, in short – are Jeff Koons' stock-in-trade.

Trade, indeed, is the operative word, because consumer culture is his principal subject matter, *à la* Andy Warhol. But whereas Warhol concentrated on everyday convenience goods such as soup cans, Brillo boxes, and Coke bottles, Koons wallows in the world of luxury goods, glossy magazines, colourful package designs, gigantic billboards and – the work he's most reviled for – scaled-up versions of tacky touristy knick-knacks, plus plastic day-glo kiddie kitsch. If Warhol is Wal-Mart in excelsis, the Koonster is Cartier, Krug, and Chloé incarnate. "Salespeople," he famously announced, "are on the front line of culture." Jeff Koons is not only on the front line of salespeople, he sells salespeople successfully to a sceptical art world audience.

But then again, he is a natural. Born in York, Pennsylvania, the only son of a furniture-store owner, our prodigy pitchman earned extra pocket money by selling gift wrapping and chocolates door to door. He bought in bulk, added a 100 percent mark-up and laughed all the way to his piggy-bank. After graduation, he moved to New York in 1977, where he got a job in the marketing department of MoMA. He sold memberships and, in classic supersize-me tradition, discovered a facility for talking people into purchasing top-dollar, high-margin museum membership packages. So successful was he that a Wall Street commodities dealer poached him for brokers Smith Barney, where serious money could be made by sellers of stocks and bonds.

Koons used these riches to underwrite his early work, which was a nod to that American archetype and formative element of his provincial upbringing, the door-to-door salesman. His first show, *The New*, comprised a series of plexiglas-encased vacuum cleaners: retail display meets readymade. Koons was instantly hailed the next big post-Pop thing. Similar raptures greeted *Equilibrium*, a 1985 installation of water-filled glass cabinets containing partly submerged basketballs alongside brass casts of life-saving equipment (aqualung, snorkel, dinghy) and framed reproductions of a Nike advertising campaign. However, it was in his next show, *Luxury and Degradation*, that Koons really got in touch with his inner marketer. Sleek magazine advertisements for Bacardi rum, Hennessy brandy, Dewar's scotch, and Gordon's gin lined the walls; silvered souvenir shop gewgaws stood on plinths; and a stainless-steel cast of a toy train that started life as a window display for Jim Beam whiskey occupied centre stage.[30]

Having thus acquired a taste for tat, Jeff Koons' confrontation with consumer culture reached its acme in the late 1980s when he assembled the vast array of oversized kitsch objects, tourist collectibles, and airport art – ceramic Yorkshire terriers, porcelain bear and policeman, inflatable rabbit in stainless steel – for which he is best known. The epitome of this endorsement of ersatz was *Michael Jackson and Bubbles*, a life-size statue of the wacko one resplendent in his finest P. T. Barnum uniform and surmounted by a replica of his pet monkey. As if that weren't disconcerting enough, Koons promptly embraced hard-core pornography under the expert tuition of his then wife, Italian skin-flick superstar and sometime politician La Cicciolina.

The ensuing eroto-show, 1992's *Made in Heaven*, was an eye-opener in more ways than one. Nevertheless, the porn-art exhibition elevated Koons to a level of superstardom that Damien Hirst can only dream about. Everything he has done since commands worldwide attention, occupies the most prestigious gallery spaces, and fetches prices that are almost as inflated as his ginormous plastic flowers in stainless steel, huge Highland terrier topiary installation *Puppy*, which guards the entrance to the Guggenheim Museum in Bilbao, and *Easy-fun-Ethereal*, billboard-sized oil paintings of computer-manipulated collages of glossy magazine advertisements. The last of these so outraged one of the photographers whose work was misappropriated – Andrea Blanch, creator of "Silk sandals by Gucci" – that she sued the Koonster for plagiarism, only to lose on the grounds of fair use. The free publicity didn't do Jeff any harm either.

As Generation X spokesperson Douglas Coupland rightly notes, you either "get" Jeff Koons or you don't. Some consider his work banal, trivial, meaningless, derivative post-PopArt pap, a tacky take on tourist tat, an affront to the great tradition. Others consider it ironic, amusing, a kitschy commodified critique of our kitschy commodified world, one where art is increasingly embracing the market. They point to the enormous inflated balloon dog that echoes the stock-market bubbles of the late twentieth century. They point to his kitschier-than-kitsch critiques of the art world in the time-honoured tradition of Duchamp and Warhol. They point to his self-promoting, self-branding behaviour – surely tongue-in-cheek – such as taking out full-page ads for himself in leading art magazines, complete with glamorous models and Ralph Lauren–alike outfits. They point to his work with Stella McCartney, whose 2005 Paris collection was based on Jeff's iconic images. They point to his uncritical endorsement of selling, advertising, marketing, and commercial life in general. Surely he's making a statement ... or taking the piss.

Koons never lets on. Deadpan, he denies any ironic intent. "I believe in advertising and media completely," he says. The art world being what it is, however, statements denying irony and advocating advertising are taken ironically too, as a kind of double-bluff. Koons can't lose, in other words. Those who like him see a wonderful post-ironic sensibility. Those who hate him see a flimflam man in thrall to repulsive consumer culture. Both nevertheless agree with Gordon Burn that Koons "is one of the great showman promoters of the past twenty years." Damien Hirst can flog a dead shark for all he's worth, but takes real genius to make a mint out of a mound of playdo.

Appropriately, the best insight into Jeff Koons' sales technique can be found in the long-running UK television campaign for Ronseal woodstains and varnishes. No-nonsense, straight-to-camera sales pitches, the ads climax with a salt-of-the-earth spokesperson holding up the product and declaring "It does exactly what it says on the tin." The ingenuity of Ronseal's campaign is that it works on two levels: as a good old-fashioned buy-this-product approach, and, for today's marketing-literate audiences, as a tongue-in-cheek take on good old-fashioned buy-this-product approaches. It's impossible to tell whether it's an unspeakably crude sales pitch or an extremely cunning one. It's both.

Whatever else is said about him, Jeff Koons' finest medium is Ronseal. Not your bog-standard Ronseal, admittedly. Top-of-the-range Ronseal. Gold-label Ronseal. Ronseal deluxe. Koonseal, in fact.

TREVOR BEATTIE (1958–)
Pimp My Brand

In the mid-1920s, Edward L. Bernays – the "L" was an affectation, by the way – was approached by the Multiple Sclerosis Society. Their name, they believed, was holding them back. It was too much of a mouthful. They wanted a change and needed the great public relations guru's sagacious advice. Bernays' solution was simplicity itself. He suggested the initials MS. Out of the mouths of babes and PR people ...

Trevor Beattie's name was also immortalized by a set of unforgettable initials. The adman extraordinary was hired in the late 1990s by a nondescript UK apparel chain called French Connection. Squeezed by high street giants such as Top Shop, Gap, Next, Principles, and the like, it was stuck in mid-market mediocrity with neither the marketing budget nor the buying clout to break through to household-name status.

Racking his brains for an edgy idea that'd catapult an anonymous client – French Connection, in case you've forgotten – to the big league of British retailing, Beattie had a Bernays-style "Big Think" moment while reading an internal memorandum that called the company by its arresting initials, FCUK.

Result!

As eureka experiences go, Beattie's memo-moment hardly qualifies as an impious Archimedes occasion. But there's no doubt that the almost-offensive acronym was the making of French Connection. When plastered on enormous billboards in busy city centres, the strapline "Fcuk fashion" stopped traffic, turned heads, prompted double-takes, and generated sufficient controversy, consternation, and comments of the well-I-never!-what-on-earth?-disgusted-Tunbridge-Wells kidney to necessitate the intervention of the British advertising watchdog.

Officially censured by the Advertising Standards Authority, the company replied with a "Fcuk advertising" billboard. Cue street cred to die for. Cue seriously soaring profits. Cue a place in the pantheon of PR stunts. Better yet, the entire cost of the £1.5 million advertising campaign was covered by the sale of 500,000 "Fcuk fashion" T-shirts.

Beginning as it intended to go on, French Connection quickly squeezed every conceivable variation out of its unforgettable acronym. Fcuk me, fcuk fear, fcuk off, fcuk FM, and fcuk Santa all had their moment in the fcukin' sun. The deathless initials were plastered on everything from fcuk deodorant and fcuk lingerie to the company's flagship store, "the biggest fcuk in the world." Sales space doubled, turnover burgeoned, America was colonized, and everyone wanted a slice of the fcuk action, even Boots the Chemist, which stocked a range of fcuk toiletries and fcuk cosmetics, though it drew the line at fcuk condoms.[31] Heaven only knows what Jesse Boot, the company's Puritan founder, would've made of it all. Fcukin' hell.

Hell indeed was where fcuk finished up. In classic Icarus brand fashion, the company crashed and burned in five short years. A joke can be told only so many times, and fcuk wore out its welcome faster than most. By 2004, it was well and truly fcuked.

Still, if ever an advertising campaign epitomized the 1990s in Great Britain, an era of post-postfeminist, non-new-man laddishness, it was surely fcuk. Only one other campaign came close and that too sprang hydra-like from the fertile head of Trevor Beattie, ladman extraordinary. A chippy working-class chap from Birmingham, Beattie hailed from a family of motor mechanics. However, his prepubescent passion for advertising jingles – he collected them like stamps – suggested that van pimping's loss would be brand pimping's gain.[32]

The first from his family to enter further education, Trev studied graphic design and photography at Wolverhampton Poly. A kindly lecturer encouraged him to enter a competition sponsored by a leading London ad agency and he scooped a creative scholarship. Within a year, by all accounts, he had reinvented Weetabix as bovver boys' breakfast cereal of choice. This was followed by sterling work for Liquorice Allsorts, intimating that eating too many turned consumers into Bertie Bassett look-alikes, and Felix cat food, whose echoic slogan "Cats like Felix like Felix" is preferred by eight out of ten admen who expressed a preference.

But by far the best of Beattie's pre-FCUK work was for Wonderbra. The "Hello boys" campaign of 1994, which displayed supermodel Eva Herzigova's assets to best advantage, gave a whole new meaning to in-your-face advertising, effectively inaugurated the mid-1990s boom in ladvertising, and not only earned Beattie the undying gratitude of every hyperventilating British bachelor but stimulated all manner of copycat-cum-parody campaigns, not least Billy Connolly's "Hello girls" riposte for Kaliber low-alcohol lager.

The wunderbar Wonderbra episode was not without professional blowback, however. Beattie was accused of taking credit for others' ideas. The copywriter behind the original poster had left Beattie's agency by the time the campaign broke. So TB stepped in to handle the accompanying publicity and collect the industry awards. In fairness, Trev was responsible for the remainder of the campaign – penning plangent slogans like "Pull yourself together" and "Or are you just pleased to see me?" – but accusations of strapline larceny tend to stick, even when entirely unwarranted.

For example, the "burglar Beattie" canard reappeared with French Connection because Beattie took credit for a company-composed acronym. It reared its ugly head again with his "Live to loaf" campaign for Strongbow cider because the slogan had previously been coined for a laid-back, take-life-easy magazine called *The Idler* (a strapline, clearly, that they take extremely seriously). Indeed, no matter how many innovative projects Beattie orchestrates, such as his surreal David Lynch–directed work for Playstation 2, his "Av it" ads for John Smith's bitter, or his classic McCain oven chips campaign (which started with a staged search for the company's "lost" promotional film and culminated in the longest-ever advert on terrestrial television), insinuations of unprofessional behaviour are never far behind. Such is the fate of creative artists from Shakespere and Picasso to W. B. Yeats and J. K. Rowling.

Controversy, then, has dogged Trevor Beattie. His work for the Labour party in particular has set the cat among the political pigeons. William Hague, the follicle-free leader of Her Majesty's loyal opposition, was portrayed as a closet wig-wearer during the general election campaign of 2001. A Maggie Thatcher wig-wearer, let it be said. Come the general election campaign of 2005, the replacement leader of Her Majesty's loyal opposition, Michael Howard, was duly depicted as a flying pig, as was his colleague, Oliver Letwin. This depiction was widely interpreted as an anti-Semitic slur, Beattie briefly became the Mel Gibson of adland, and he resigned as chairman of TBWA not long after. The two events are totally unrelated, Your Honour.

Clever Trevor has since set up his own agency, Beattie McGuinness Bungay – the last of the three is presumably a tongue-in-cheek reference to H. G. Wells' finest marketing creation – from whence he pours scorn on the parlous state of the advertising industry. Once the envy of the world, UK advertisers are increasingly pandering to the knuckle-dragging demands of clients rather than producing the kind of campaigns that Beattie is famous for. "The quality of advertising has never been lower," he announced in 2005. "Most of the ads on TV now aren't good enough and no one seems to care. No one's ranting about the fact that everyone's ads suck. Because they're all taking the shilling for doing it; compromising for fear they'll lose the business."

Compromise is not part of Trevor Beattie's vocabulary, nor is fear of failure. His latest venture is a kind of anti-advertising

advertising agency. "I've read a lot of stuff," he says, "about what I'm supposed to be doing. Everyone is telling me we're not an ad agency and we're going to be producing art and sculpture and sending men to the moon. It's quite nice in a way ... So we'll try some things. I'm not afraid of failing. The key is: how do you make it pay?"

It remains to be seen whether Trevor will hit anti-marketing pay-dirt. But in a world of smarmy, smooth-talking, sharp-suited, establishment-stroking, don't-bite-the-hand back-slapping, Beattie remains an unreconstructed class warrior, with a thick Brummie accent, a penchant for public transport, and a look that's one part Richard Branson jeans 'n' jumper to two parts Kevin Keegan bubble perm. That's the radical retro image he presents, anyway. He's the antithesis of Charles Saatchi, the polar opposite of Martin Sorrell, nothing less than the anti-Ogilvy of advertising. Whereas David Ogilvy was as smooth as a shaved peach, Trevor Beattie's look is as rough as the proverbial badger's bum. Whereas David Ogilvy was research-led and rules-based, Trevor Beattie is insanely intuitive and enthusiasm-driven. Whereas David Ogilvy wrote the book that keeps his memory green, Trevor Beattie eschews personal publicity and publicizes this eschewal incessantly. Edward L. Bernays would be proud of him.

GABRIELLE CHANEL (1883–1971)
Coco Says No

Coco must be turning in her grave. Elegantly, of course. Imperiously, even.

The cause of her consternation? That television ad for Chanel Number 5. You know the one. The one starring Nicole Kidman. The one that's an echo of *Moulin Rouge*, with star-crossed lovers. The one directed, at mind-boggling expense, by Baz Luhrmann. The one that's so over the top it's almost in orbit. Around Saturn. In a parallel universe.

Chanel, you see, was a minimalist. She eschewed ostentation. She made her name by spurning Edwardian excess. She rejected the corseted, constricted, cantilevered couture of *la belle époque*. Avoidance of elaboration marks her most famous creations: the little black dress, the fitted jacket, the two-piece suit, the two-tone shoe. Her look, in short, was so severely classical it makes Ancient Rome look rococo.

You only have to consider Chanel Number 5 to see what I mean. The bottle is simple, solid, square, chunky, the modernist architecture of Le Corbusier in miniature. Striking today, its austerity was even more conspicuous in 1921, a time when perfumes were sold in fanciful ornamental flaçons and came complete with extravagantly romantic brand names like Coeur en Folie, Mille et Une Nuits, or La Fille de Roi du Chine. Chanel Number 5 announced its difference not simply by the unusual numeral or the minimalist aesthetic of the boxy bottle, but by the fact that it was an unashamedly synthetic scent in a world of precious pressed-flower extracts. It was a perfect symbol of the machine age, then at its height.

But what, I hear you ask, happened to Numbers 1 through 4? Ah, that would be telling. As with many iconic brands, there are numerous nativity narratives. The number 5 refers to

Coco's birthday. (Not true.) Five was her lucky number. (Quite correct, though it became her favourite after 5's success, not before.) It was the fifth sample out of eight prepared for her by ace perfumier Ernest Beaux. (Hmmm. Who am I to scotch a legend, let alone the rumour that Coco was introduced to Beaux by one of the killers of Rasputin, Grand Duke Dmitri Pavlovich? Just think, if Charles Revson sold eau d'assignation, Coco Chanel sold eau d'assassination.)

What, you didn't know about the Rasputin connection? There's a lot you don't know about Gabrielle Chanel:

1. Coco was a stage name acquired during her stint as a cabaret singer. An illegitimate child, she was abandoned when her father ran off after her mother's sudden death. Shipped to a nun-run orphanage in Aubazine, Gabrielle learned to sew – and not much else – amid grim surroundings.[33] At eighteen, she moved to the garrison town of Moulins, where she worked in a lingerie emporium and moonlighted as a cabaret singer. What she lacked in vocal dexterity she compensated with personal charisma, proving popular with the officers and men. Her repertoire was limited, however. It consisted of two songs "*Ko ko ri ko*" and "*Qui a vu Coco?*" Hence the nickname.

2. A termination was her entrée to entrepreneurialism. She fell pregnant to an officer of the Tenth Light Horse, Etienne Balsan, who arranged an abortion, then illegal. He also introduced her to the high-society horsey set. Coco was a quick study and soon picked up the mores of his upper-crust equestrian circle. Her self-made millinery caused a sensation at race meetings, where large hats were *de rigueur*. She was asked about her creations so often that going into the chapeau business seemed a smart move. Balsan bankrolled her first retail outlet in his Paris apartment on Boulevard Malesherbes.

3. She owed everything to a Geordie. One of Balsan's aristo-
    cratic acquaintances, Arthur "Boy" Capel, fell for the dark-
    haired ingénue. The eldest son of an affluent industrialist
    with extensive coal-mining interests in north-east England,
    Boy played polo when not attending to the family busi-
    ness. He provided the funding for her first boutique proper,
    in the street that would for ever be associated with Chanel,
    rue Cambon. Boy also underwrote her second outlet, in the
    upmarket holiday resort of Deauville. It was there that the
    Chanel look made its debut in the summer of 1913. Her
    casual sports- and beach-wear, the antithesis of bustles,
    corsets, stiff collars, and constrictive corsage, proved
    enormously popular with the beautiful people who packed
    Deauville for the season.

4. Coco was a Ritz cracker. She was in the right place at the
    right time: Deauville in the lazy hazy days of 1913 and,
    even more so, rue Cambon during the First World War. Her
    boutique was next door to the rear entrance of the Ritz
    Hotel, just about the only building in Paris untroubled by
    wartime shortages of winter heating fuel. It was the fash-
    ionable meeting-place of society ladies, and the House of
    Chanel benefited by proximity. The pared-down, minimal-
    ist, masculine look of her collections also connected with
    a wartime ethos in which women were making their pres-
    ence felt in occupations formerly dominated by men.
    Functional chic was in and Chanel's *miserabilisme de luxe*
    was in with it.

5. Chanel comforted a tearful Churchill. The interwar years
    were Coco's finest hour – LBD, Number 5, collarless cardi-
    gan suits, the so-called *garçonne* look (what we term the
    flapper). But you already know that. They were also the
    years of her dalliance with one of England's wealthiest
    men, the Duke of Westminster. Winston Churchill was a
    personal friend, what's more, as were the *crème de la*

crème of European society. During the abdication crisis of
1936 when Winston's best buddy Edward VIII was determined to stand by Wallis Simpson, the British bulldog
wept uncontrollably in Coco's arms. Mind you, as Wallis
Simpson wasn't one of her customers, our fashion führer
shed few sympathetic tears in return.[34]

You learn something new every day, eh? Well, there are five
more things you should know, as marketers, about the irascible, incorrigible, incomparable Coco Chanel:

1. Her attitude to clients was one of animosity verging on
    abhorrence. Even though she was couturier to many of the
    European elite, countless titled aristocrats among them,
    Chanel seldom served her customers personally. She dealt
    with them through underlings. "A client seen," one of her
    celebrated maxims went, "is a client lost." By making
    herself inaccessible, she piqued customers' curiosity and
    boosted her own marketing mystique. Coco didn't listen to
    her customers either, not even indirectly. She dictated
    what fashion would be. She sensed that many women were
    bewildered by a surfeit of choice and wanted to be told
    what to wear. So she imperiously announced what was
    what, and during her glory years between the wars every-
    one who was anyone fell into line. In those days of filter-
    down fashion, when the well-heeled set the pace, Chanel
    trained the well-bred well. She led the horsey set to water
    and made them drink.

2. An anti-customer ethos also shaped Chanel's internal mar-
    keting campaigns, if you can call them that. Even though
    she came from a poor provincial background and knew
    what it was like to work for a pittance as a seamstress,
    Coco treated her employees abominably. When one of her
    premières – a senior member of staff who'd been with the
    firm for ten years – asked for a modest pay rise, she was
    sacked on the spot. Chanel's 3,000 employees were grossly

underpaid, worked extremely long hours, and accommodated the capricious demands of the fashion fascist-in-command. Yet when they went on strike for better working conditions in the late thirties, she immediately closed down her atelier and fired them all *tout de suite*. Today's third-world sweatshops are oases of enlightened management practice compared to the conditions that Coco's workforce endured. To say she was as hard as nails is a gross understatement. Talons of steel, perhaps.

3.   Decades before designer-attired superstars commenced cavorting on the red carpets *du monde*, Chanel had the celebrity clotheshorse dressage down to a fine art. From the outset, she gave free outfits to high-profile society women who, when asked the name of their couturier, whispered Chanel to everyone within earshot. By the early thirties she was dressing such Hollywood stars as Gloria Swanson and receiving screen credit for her costumes. Fifty years before Giorgio Armani's much-vaunted breakthrough in *American Gigolo*, Chanel had product placement off pat. She also provided the costumes for several avant garde stage plays by Jean Cocteau, as well as for the incomparable Ballets Russes of showman supreme Sergei Diaghilev.

4.   Coco had a cavalier attitude toward copycats. Her designs were repeated and royally ripped off by fast franc-makers. Egregious imitations didn't bother her in the slightest. She regarded them as a compliment, as spontaneous publicity, as a signifier of her status as the pre-eminent trendsetter. Whereas competing fashion houses took up legal cudgels against the counterfeiters, Coco was quite relaxed about Chanelesque confections. She even pirated herself, particularly during her comeback collection of 1954. Bored after the closure of her house and seemingly stung by the stunning post-war success of Christian Dior's New Look,

she re-entered the fifties fashion fray with a huge fanfare of publicity. However, her much-hyped collection turned out to be a reprise of the classic interwar look. The fashion press in Paris loathed it, likewise the glossies in London. But New York loved the look of looks, variations on which are still extremely popular today. A star was reborn.

5. Part of the reason for Coco's dramatic comeback was a worrying decline in her principal source of post-war income. Despite the endorsement of Marilyn Monroe, who famously wore nothing in bed but Number 5, Chanel's share of the iconic perfume's licensing fees was a sore point. Though the tight-fisted designer sued her partners, she was unsuccessful and, all things considered, she made very little money from her greatest hit, the marketing of which she'd masterminded. When the very first batch of Number 5 was ready, she sprayed her fitting-rooms with the striking scent. When her high-society clients inquired about the wonderful smell, she feigned indifference, saying it was something she'd come across in Grasse and she just happened to have a few samples she could let them try. But when subsequently persuaded by enthusiastic customers, she reluctantly agreed to make her private scent more widely available (meanwhile manufacturing it in bulk). Such was the buzz about this "unique" mass-produced perfume that it was an instant success and, despite Nicole Kidman's recent efforts, remains the world's number-one-selling scent.

Now you know.

RON POPEIL (1935–)
Set It and Forget It

If at one pole of marketing accomplishment stands mighty Chanel Number 5, the perfume that every woman finds acceptable and every man can purchase with confidence, the majestic occupant of the opposite marketing pole is GLH Number 9. Beloved by the Bobby Charltons, Donald Trumps, Gerhard Schröders, and Mel Gibsons of this world – if that's not a weave, Mel, I don't know what is – GLH Number 9 is the ultimate accessory for alpha males in their declining years. Spray-on hair is not something sufferers of male-pattern baldness like to talk about, but as with athlete's foot, tennis elbow, housemaid's knee, gamer's thumb, and analogous ailments invented by marketers, MPB can be cured with a squirt or two of GLH. Great-looking hair.

When this wonder cure for male-pattern baldness was unleashed upon a waiting world in 1992, "hair in a can" attracted almost as much attention as Coco Chanel's immortal aroma. It was the Viagra of its day. A veritable marketing miracle. The revelation that it was the only thing Phil Kotler wore in bed didn't do much for sales, admittedly. But in a year where the cultural highlights were *Wayne's World*, "Achy Breaky Heart," and the election of Bill Clinton, spray-on hair stood proud, defiant, and available in nine different colours including black, white, blond, and silver-brown. Line extensions like GLH Finishing Shield and, gulp, GLH Hair Cleanser were also available to its follically challenged adherents.

The man behind GLH is Ron Popeil. Ron, in turn, is the person behind Ronco, the company behind all those unnecessary kitchen gadgets – the Chop-O-Matic, the Veg-O-Matic, the Showtime Rotisserie – you've bought in desperation as a present for that special someone who has everything, foot spa and fondue set included. They are the gadgets that seemed like a good idea at the time, usually when you were watching the shopping channel for want of anything better to do. They are the gadgets that are cluttering up your kitchen cupboards right now and that you can't bring yourself to throw out because you never know when they might come in handy.

Self-styled "salesman of the century" Ron Popeil is king of the infomercial.[35] The infomercial, in case you've forgotten the antecedents of YouTube, is the mutant marketing lovechild of talk show and commercial break. A thirty-minute sales spiel interlarded with inane interviews, audience participation, and compelling product demonstrations, it came to the fore in the early 1990s as a consequence of the cable and satellite TV revolution and attendant deregulation of TV advertising in the United States. It was a metier made for Ron Popeil. No one, but no one, could match his sales-pitch prowess. It was said he could sell nail varnish to the Venus de Milo. Hell, the man moved a million cans of GLH. Mainly to Elton John, I grant you. But give the guy some credit.

Ron Popeil's prowess is all in the genes. He came from a long line of pitchpersons. His father, S. J. Popeil, was a Depression-era huckster on the country-fair circuit, as was his uncle Raymond, as were innumerable relatives on his fraternal grandmother's side. The Morris family of Asbury Park, NJ, were bona fide boardwalk legends who could sell empty boxes and charge extra for the air rights therein. Ron, however, grew up in isolation, cut off from family influences or advice.

Abandoned by his parents as a three-year-old, he was sent to a tough boarding school in upstate New York and eventually taken in by his squabbling grandparents. Isodore, his grandfather, was a pattern-cutter in a Miami textile factory and a singularly mean-spirited individual who tied the hyperactive youngster to his bed and beat him mercilessly if he so much as moved. Soon after the war, the "family" moved to Chicago, where Ron's father and uncle had opened a factory in an insalubrious part of town. Popeil Brothers manufactured knick-knacks, gee-gaws, and extraneous kitchen gadgets for the itinerant pitchperson trade. Although Ron had no direct dealings with his estranged father, he worked in the Popeil plant at weekends for pocket money.

A failure at school, Ron embarked on his real education in 1951, when he had a Eureka moment in Maxwell Street market, the Cook County mecca of street vendors, shady dealers, and the back-of-a-lorry brigade. Popeil was transfixed. He watched what the pitchpersons were doing and knew instinctively he could do better. Much better.

Selling Popeil Brothers products, principally the phenomenal Chop-O-Matic, a multi-use slicing, dicing kitchen accoutrement, he soon became the star of the street. According to his autobiography, he was clearing $500 a week at sixteen – some going in the early 1950s and not to be sneezed at even today. In addition to the Maxwell Street market, young Popeil rampaged around the county-fair circuit cleaning up as he went, and eventually used his earnings to enrol in the University of Illinois.

Unimpressed by the groves of academe, Ron quit college after a few months, returned to the university of life, and eventually graduated with honours in hard knocks. He cut a deal with the manager of Woolworth's flagship store in downtown Chicago – this was in the days when Woolies was wonderful – and practised his patter in-store for a slice of the ensuing till action. A silver-tongued salesperson whose mesmeric performances became must-see attractions for office workers on their lunch break, Ron was earning $1,000 a week at a time when the average monthly salary was $500. You name it, he sold it. Shoeshine sprays, glass knives, plastic pot-plants, haircare requisites, and multifarious kitchen implements such as the Food Glamorizer, a gadget that performed 13 different functions from peeling carrots and carving pumpkins to removing the string from celery.

Television quickly came a-calling. By the early sixties, Ron was making commercials for Popeil Brothers products. Shown on local stations, usually in the wee small hours when airtime was cheap, these no-budget productions established the classic Ronco template. Liberally sprinkled with magic marketing words like "amazing," "miracle," "special," "free," and, naturally, "magic," Ron's rapid-fire, extra-enthusiastic, but-wait-there's-more delivery captivated all who witnessed it.

Chop-O-Matics, Veg-O-Matics, Dial-O-Matics, Peel-O-Matics, Corn-O-Matics, Mince-O-Matics, and Sledge-O-Matics were joined by countless other cheap and cheerful Popeil products. These included spray guns, cookie cutters, donut makers, orange juicers, glass frosters, air filters, miracle brushes, spiral slicers, smokeless ashtrays, bottle and jar cutters, run-resistant pantyhose, seal-a-meal packages, inside-outside window washers, inside-the-shell egg scramblers, cordless-electric power scissors, carpet cleaners, steam pressers, rhinestone setters, pottery wheels, and sewing machines, to say nothing of the unforgettable compilation albums of "top hits by original stars." Now that's what I call marketing.

Ronco's biggest hits, however, were Mr Microphone, a radio mike that broadcast the speaker's voice from appropriately tuned transistor radios; the Pocket Fisherman, a complete fishing rod and line that collapsed neatly into a pocket-sized package (albeit a fairly capacious pocket); and above all the Bass-O-Matic, a classic 1976 comedy sketch on *Saturday Night Live* in which Dan Aykroyd pitched a spoof Popeil product that liquidized a whole fish "just the way you like it."

Spurred by the *SNL* spoof, Ronco's immortal tagline "As seen on TV" rapidly entered popular culture. Buoyed by its staggering sales success, the company went public. A multimillionaire with jet-setting lifestyle to match, Ron lived a luxe-o-matic existence with the usual trophy wives, trophy mansions, trophy sailboats, and trophy trophies.

Inevitably, it all went pear-shaped. Ronco collapsed in 1984 and the salesman of the century found himself back on the county-fair circuit, pitch-o-matic on overdrive. Having acquired the entire inventory of his bankrupt company at a rock-bottom price, Ron sold it all off in three years flat.

Semi-retired and all but exhausted, Ron fell into the welcome embrace of Las Vegas wonder-worker Steve Wynn, who was endeavouring to upgrade the down-at-heel resort. Ron joined the board of Mirage Casino and recharged his marketing batteries as the eighties segued into the nineties. Then came the shopping-channel revolution. Thirty-minute infomercials were the perfect vehicle for old-school pitchpersons – infinitely superior to the rapid-fire two-minute TV commercials of the seventies – and Popeil took to the medium like the proverbial duck to crispy batter. Dehydrators, rotisseries, pasta makers, retro re-issues of Ronco's much-loved classics, and above all the indescribable GLH Number 9 soon put Popeil back on top. Thin on top, yes, but the pitchman's pitchman reclaimed his crown. And then some.

So what, I hear you ask, is the secret of pitch-perfect sales spiels? Luckily, Timothy Samuelson has studied them for us and it seems that the classic Popeilite palaver consists of nine elements: 1) select a high-traffic location; 2) build a crowd and hold their attention; 3) make the product sound indispensable while describing its attributes and demonstrating its features; 4) emphasize its usefulness again and again ... and again; 5) pepper the patter with "the most fantastic," "... incredible," "... amazing" and sundry other superlatives; 6) include the audience by asking rhetorical questions or exchanging good-natured banter; 7) convey the price of the product, usually via some version of the countdown technique: not $10, or $8, or $6, or even $4, but an incredible, one-time-only $3; 8) before you take the money that purchasers are by now eagerly pressing on you, add a free, bonus, no-extra-charge product to the package; 9) collect the cash from all but a small group of very keen customers, promising them something else so as to form the core of the crowd that you'll work in the next iteration of Popeil-O-Matic marketing.

But, wait, there's more ...

MASON LOCKE WEEMS (1760–1825)
Book-Peddling Parson

Far from being a marketing backwater as some suggest, the book trade has always been a bubbling wellspring of commercial creativity. Many bestselling authors began their careers in the marketing trenches: F. Scott Fitzgerald, Fay Weldon, Salman Rushdie, Kurt Vonnegut, Peter Carey, Dorothy L. Sayers, Tom Clancy, Elmore Leonard, Monica Ali, Augusten Burroughs, to name but a few. Many other authors have possessed a natural flair for selling despite their lack of formal training in the art of authorpreneurship: Alexandre Dumas, Charles Dickens, Mark Twain, L. Frank Baum, Edgar Rice Burroughs, Norman Mailer, and of late J. K. Rowling. Numerous editors and bookpersons, moreover, have been blessed with abundant marketing skills: Henry Colburn, the so-called "prince of puffers" in Victorian London; Harold Livemore, the great jazz-age literary impresario; Allen Lane, the brains behind the pick-up-a-Penguin paperback revolution of the 1930s; and Jack McClelland, the Canadian showman-shaman of the 1960s who was never loth to push his wares in larger-than-life fashion.

None of these compares with Mason Locke Weems. Today the peerless parsonpreneur is best remembered for his infamous *Life of George Washington*. Published in 1800, this was the biography that introduced the cherry-tree-meets-hatchet incident in which a callow father of the nation confessed his inability to tell lies. Though recycled on countless occasions thereafter, the lie story was itself a lie. A whopper, in fact. But then again, the one and only Weems was never averse to coming up with a "stretcher." Truth may be the first casualty of war, but it is ripped limb from limb in the killing fields of commerce.

Son of an Ulster-Scots immigrant, Mason Locke Weems was born in Maryland on 11 October 1859, the youngest of nineteen children.[36] After studying medicine in Edinburgh and fighting in the American War of Independence, he concluded that saving souls was his true calling. Ordained by the Bishop of Chester in 1784, Weems reported for duty at Herring Creek, Maryland, where he was appointed rector of All Hallows parish. However, the lost sheep of Herring Creek didn't take to the bumptious young preacher, who was a bit too radical for their liking. He refused to condemn Methodists as the spawn of the devil and was prone to passionate displays of oratory when pontificating from the pulpit. That would never do in a community that liked its religion unvarnished, unadulterated, uncontaminated – preferably straight from the pale horse's mouth, so to speak.

Disliked by fellow clergymen, who despaired of his "diabolical spirit," Weems had a career ladder with very few rungs, widely spaced and liable to collapse when weight was applied. Thus he was forced to supplement his income by selling sermons. As copyright laws didn't yet exist, Weems indulged in a bit of illegal downloading. He persuaded a local printer to knock off an anthology of a British preacher's greatest hits and sold them on his travels around the countryside, recruiting clerical colleagues as sellers of subscriptions. Stuffy sermons didn't sell well, unfortunately. So he turned his hand to what we would consider Christmas stocking-fillers: little self-help books of apt quotations, stirring stories, edifying folk wisdom, and personal-development parables. Chicken soup for the soul, in short. These included *Twelve Cents' Worth of Wit* and *Little Stories for Little Folk of All Denominations*. Little sales as well. The kid-lit market wasn't ready for Weems. Not at 12 cents a pop.

Churchless after 1791, Mason Locke Weems hawked his tracts around Maryland and Chesapeake while soliciting subscriptions for the unsuccessful sermons series. He went for broke with his next book, *Onania*, which warned readers of "the heinous sin of self-pollution and all its fearful consequences in both sexes." This allegedly uplifting book was more talked about than read and more read than bought, since copies of the salacious text were passed samizdat-like among God-fearing, sin-ridden, onanistically inclined colonials. The fact that it was penned by a parson only added to its lubricious lure. Pulpitporn!

In terms of hard sales, however, *Onania*'s commercial sperm-count was lamentable. Literary IVF was required, and the voluptuary vicar came good with a fifteenth-century guide to good health written by an Italian nobleman. The Trevor Beattie of his day, Weems shamelessly plundered Luigi Cornaro's classic text, albeit interlarding it with his own sage advice on healthy lifestyles. His Chesapeake Bay Diet was predicated, as are most diets, on the avoidance of gluttony. Quoting Ecclesiastes, the ex-minister exhorted eighteenth-century junk-food addicts to "go forth and puke." Failure to do so, he further warned, caused "general heaviness and weariness of body, flatulent uneasiness, frequent eructations," together with "disturbed slumber" and "frightful dreams." Tell me about it.

Like a Yankee Jamie Oliver, Mason Locke Weems drummed up support for his New World regimen. He sent a signed copy of the book, suitably retitled *The Immortal Mentor*, to George Washington himself, who replied with a boilerplate letter of thanks. Weems interpreted this as celebrity endorsement and retailed the book thereafter with an "as recommended by" screamer. It was reprinted on countless occasions, sold well for nigh on twenty years, and, more important, established the admonitory tone that characterized Weems' subsequent bestsellers.

The mid-1790s did more than establish the writer's singular literary voice. They also witnessed his alliance with Mathew Carey, an energetic Irish immigrant who acquired a failing

Philadelphia publishing operation and set out to make his name as a bookman. With Weems' assistance, he did so. Although Weems wasn't his only salesperson, or even salesparson, he was the indefatigable marketing maestro who carried Carey to the top tier of the American book trade.

Supplied with Carey's extensive catalogue of bibles, chapbooks, romances, plays, almanacs, hymnals, spelling books, and so forth, Weems sallied forth with a wagon and sold, sold, sold all over the antebellum South. This was the great age of the Yankee pedlar, and few peddled further or faster than Weems. Although retail stores existed in many communities, itinerant wagons filled with fold-out display counters offered a much wider range of books at more attractive prices. They were the Amazon of their day, and Weems was their Bezos. Only more ebullient.

The book-peddling parson's success wasn't solely attributable to his energetic coverage of the southern states, commendably tireless though that was. Nor was it a consequence of his slightly shady reputation, though this former man of the cloth attracted the curious, the censorious, and the craven scandal-seeker. Nor was it caused by the racy titles of his stock-in-trade – *The Lover's Almanac*, *The Bachelor's Almanac*, or that unfortunate flop *Onania* – though sex always sells, as our pulpitporn purveyor well knew. No, Mason Locke Weems was a wizard at drumming up business. He timed his community calls impeccably: after church, post-harvest, during festivities, indeed at any time or place where a crowd was sure to be gathering.

If there wasn't a crowd, he'd assemble one himself. A talented fiddle player, he entertained his prospects with stirring tunes before launching into his sales spiel. He complemented the toe-tappers with side-splitters, since he was also a disarmingly funny raconteur. When sales were sluggish, he launched into a funny walk rather like Charlie Chaplin's celebrated drunkard routine. If all else failed, he fell back on his original calling and officiated at weddings, funerals and other rites. Naturally, he took the opportunity to recommend a few uplifting or comforting titles that he just happened to have on his parson person.

It's easy at our present remove to disparage Weems' remarkable marketing achievements or to assume that he was pushing at an open door. Rapidly growing population, ever-increasing literacy, steadily advancing affluence, slowly improving communications networks, and the religious revivals of the early nineteenth century all boded well for the book-selling parson. But it's important to appreciate that books were expensive luxuries, something that farming communities could ill afford, and that the territory was far from virgin. Weems' biggest sellers were bibles. However, just about every family back then already possessed a bible or several. They didn't need another. They didn't want another. But that never stopped a supersalesman. Carey couldn't keep up with the demand that his pitch-perfect pitchman produced.

Indeed, when Carey wouldn't deliver what Weems wanted, the pushy parson penned and published the blighters himself. Having found his literary voice with *The Immortal Mentor*, he cranked out all sorts of uplifting pamphlets: *The Drunkard's Looking-Glass*, *The Bad Wife's Looking-Glass*, *God's Revenge Against Adultery*, *God's Revenge Against Gambling*, *God's Revenge Against Murder*, and the ever-popular *Hymen's Recruiting Sergeant*, a kind of nineteenth-century *Joy of Sex*. As a rule, these works of "moral sensationalism" featured gory details of the aberrant behaviours at issue combined with uplifting guidelines as to how the wanton wickedness could be avoided.[37] Naturally, the gory details were described at greater length than the uplifting antidotes. Much greater.

The gory details, what's more, came wrapped in prose so purple it almost qualifies as indigo. Even Gabriele d'Annunzio at his most poetic couldn't match the book-peddling parson in full flight. And nowhere did he let fly more fully than in his stretcher-stuffed *Life of Washington*, which he sold assiduously throughout his life. It has sold steadily since. With the exception of Franklin's *Autobiography*, it is the only book of the period that's still in print. How many marketing creations outlive their creators by two centuries?

DONALD TRUMP (1946–)
A Rug as Big as the Ritz

Several years ago, I wrote a book called *Free Gift Inside!!* In it, I sang the praises of one Donald John Trump, trickster supreme. At the time of writing, The Donald was in deep trouble. His Atlantic City casinos were losing money faster than Richard Hammond's Vampire at take-off. The idea for a reality TV show based on business challenges hadn't yet occurred to Trump, though many were telling him "You're fired!" He was being written off as a fading relic of the buccaneering 1980s, with hairdo to match. But there was something about his three-scoops comb-over – GLH perhaps – that told me The Donald would rise again.[38]

Now, a comb-over, even one as baroque as Trump's, may seem an irrational rationale for expressing confidence in a business executive. Yet it occurs to me that just as manners maketh man, so too coiffures maketh marketers. You can tell much about a salesperson by their appearance in general and their hairdo in particular. Pompadours, bouffants, beehives, and just about anything that falls into the big hair category is a sure sign of huckster at work. You have been warned.

In this regard, Donald's comb-over as big as the Ritz warrants induction in the tonsorial hall of fame, or possibly even being carved into the marketing equivalent of Mount Rushmore. It was always on the cards, of course. Donald was a marketer from day one. The son of an affluent New York property developer who made a fortune out of tract houses in the outer suburbs, Donald was sent to a military academy where buzz-cuts were the norm and uniforms *de rigueur*. Today's dark-blue suits, crisp white shirts, bright-red Windsor-knotted ties, and copper-coloured confection on top are a direct descendent of The Donald's school uniform, as is his commercial acumen.

He showed a flair for business at school, studied economics at Wharton, and went into the family business on graduation.

Building penny-ante walk-ups in the 'burbs, however, held little attraction for our ambitious real-estate impresario, especially when the core of the Big Apple was so close. The Donald's first foray into Gotham's property market was a classic case of right time, right place, right hairdo. In the late seventies, the City Hall of the city that never sleeps was suffering sleepless nights over underinvestment. In an attempt to attract venture capitalists, the almost insolvent conurbation offered tax concessions to the foolhardy few who were prepared to sink millions into the Manhattan money pit.

Supported by his father, Trump plunged into the abyss of destiny. He redeveloped the bankrupt Commodore Hotel, an art deco masterpiece, and refurbished the Wollman Skating Rink in Central Park. The latter had become something of a *bête noir* for New Yorkers. Work on the two-year, $2.5 million project had started in 1980, but six years and $12 million later it still wasn't finished. The Donald offered to do the job for buttons, was rebuffed by City Hall bureaucrats, and found himself idolized in the press as an urban philanthropist – the Mother Theresa of real estate. When finally awarded the contract after a prolonged media campaign, he not only did the job inside six months and below budget, but used the remaining funds to refit an adjacent ice-skate storage facility.

Viewed in retrospect, the $3 million Wollman project seems trivial, a peanut-button rehab of a rickety ice rink. But it was The Donald's springboard to superstardom. It established the Trump brand in one fell swoop. It gave him incredible name recognition in the then low-profile world of wheeler-dealer property development. It gave him leverage in a market where leverage is crucial: a market awash with investors, venture capitalists, zoning officials, and other core components of the real-estate sudoku. Pre-Wollman, The Donald was a bumptious big-haired braggart. Post-Wollman, he was NYC's commercial-property sudoku champion, as well as a bumptious big-haired braggart. What's not to like?

Wollman also drew attention to Trump Tower, The Donald's glitzy Fifth Avenue showcase. It in turn pump-primed copious Trump-themed property development projects from condos to casinos, to say nothing of airlines, hotels, country clubs, golf courses, beauty pageants, sports promotions, and alleged adventures in greenmail. Before long, Trump became a byword – buyword rather – for OTT eighties excess, for the triumph of *nouveau riche* vulgarity, for a personal fortune that makes Croesus look like a panhandler, for an architectural aesthetic that can only be described as *trump l'oeil* and for the gilded giganticism that passes for good taste in the United States of Ersatz.

Boom gave way to bust, as is its wont, and the early 1990s found The Donald severely overextended. The interest payments on his loans far exceeded even what Trump's high-end casinos could charm out of high-rollers. More than 150 creditors came a-calling in 1994. Trump was on the point of shutting up shop and disappearing into the black hole of eighties nostalgia alongside power dressing, shoulder pads, yuppies, *Dynasty*, *Dirty Dancing*, *Miami Vice* and New Romantics. Then The Donald restructured his debts and came roaring back. The Trump World Tower, a residential development opposite the United Nations HQ; The Trump International Hotel & Tower at Columbus Circle; and Trump Place, a massive mixed-use development on the banks of the Hudson River, all conspired to put Trump back on top.

Hubris also made a reappearance. Our self-styled comeback king promptly tripped on another casino-constructed stumbling-block and plunged into Chapter 11 in 2002. Then, happy day, *The Apprentice* hoved into view. Despite predictions of humiliating failure, the reality TV show was a smash hit, as was its producer, presenter, and principal beneficiary. It remains so. The king of kitsch is back and leveraging his brand name like nobody's business. Bottled water, business suits, mortgage provision, personal finance, executive travel (Go Trump), and intellectual leadership (Trump Big Think Expo) are his latest escapades. Ya gotta love him!

Comb-over apart, what's the secret of Trump's triumph? That's a no-brainer if ever there was one, because the tycoon has told us how he does it. On page 166 of *The Art of the Deal*, one of his many bestselling autobiographies, The Donald reveals all: "Our marketing strategy was to play hard to get. It was a reverse sales technique. If you sit in an office with a contract in your hand, eager to make the first deal that comes along, it's quite obvious to people that the apartments aren't in demand. We were never in a rush to sign a contract. When people came in, we'd show them the model apartments, sit down and talk, and, if they were interested, explain that there's a waiting list for the most desirable apartments. The more unattainable the apartments seemed, the more people wanted them."[39]

Trump, in short, realizes that selling stuff doesn't involve kow-towing to customers of any kind, be they merchant banks, construction firms, local government officers, casino-licensing commissions, or, as in the instance just cited, would-be purchasers of luxury apartments in Trump Tower. The Donald delights in making life difficult for the customer. His brinkmanship is legendary. His negotiating skills are unsurpassed. He has an uncanny ability to size up clients and opponents alike. He is a master of strategic tantrum-throwing. He has no time for fancy marketing surveys or sycophantic MBAs from Harvard, Wharton, or where have you.

The Donald, what's more, is a master of "truthful hyperbole." Everything he does is bigger, better, higher, longer, greater, further, classier, or richer than has ever gone before. He has his name on more Manhattan buildings than McDonald's. His ego is so enormous that it takes crampons, oxygen, and sherpas just to scale the lower foothills. He's played

Trumpy-pumpy with innumerable pneumatic supermodels, photogenic strumpets, and assorted Trumptotty, or so his priapic press-clippings suggest. His idea of corporate social responsibility is to reduce his consumption of extra-hold hairspray out of concern for the hole in the ozone layer, the discovery of which, curiously enough, coincided with the rise of The Donald.

This combination of chutzpah and counter-customer-centricity is hard to beat, as numerous incidents from his autobiographies attest. Apparently, he persuaded the owners of the Commodore Hotel to announce its closure, which bounced City Hall into making financial concessions to the then penniless developer. Apparently, his architectural models of Trump Tower were so grotesque that the owner of Tiffany, renowned aesthete Walter Hoving, sold him the air rights over the Fifth Avenue flagship to enable him to build a better-looking edifice. Apparently, he duped Holiday Inns into thinking that his Atlantic City casino was under construction by the simple expedient of hiring every bulldozer and dump truck in town and making them look busy while the suits looked on. Apparently, he outmanoeuvred the honest burghers of Palm Beach, played zoning poker with the town council, and succeeded in turning his 128-room mansion Mar-a-Lago into an exclusive retreat for A-list celebrities.

In the early 1990s, what's more, when things were looking especially grim, The Donald repeatedly threatened to declare himself bankrupt, which would have precipitated a blizzard of intractable inter-bank litigation. From this paradoxical position of strength, the great negotiator extracted incredible concession after incredible concession from his irate creditors. He did likewise in 2002 when his casinos hit the skids.

Post-*Apprentice*, however, the word is his oyster. What price a move into haircare requisites (Trump Trichology), perfume (Trump Toilet Water), personal wellbeing (Trump Tan), or massage parlours (Trump Hump)? What price a move into the market for less prestigious accommodation (Trump Tenement, Trump Terrace, Trump Trailer Park, Trump Two-up Two-down, Trump Thatched Cottage with feature comb-over roof)? Hell, why stop at comb-over cottages? An entire community is possible – let's call it Trump Town or Trumpton – complete with cemeteries (Trump Tomb), newspapers (*Trump Times*), restaurants (Trump Trattoria), petrol stations (Trump Pump), public houses (Trump Tavern), waste-disposal facilities (Trump Dump). Sod it, why stop at Trumpton? Planet Trump's a possibility, surely.

Actually, if all else fails, he could do a Madonna and write uplifting children's literature. *Trumplestiltskin*'s first in line, presumably.

MADONNA (1958–)
Confessions on a Sales Floor

Kids. I don't know. On the one hand, you gotta love 'em. On the other hand, they're more trouble than they're worth. From a marketing perspective, that is. They can make or break a brand. The upside is not simply the staggering size of the kiddie market, which has more segments than a crateful of chocolate oranges, but also the opportunity it affords for life-long loyalty inculcation.

The downside is that the kiddie market is a morass, a swamp that's swallowed more sales campaigns than Tony the Tiger has Frosties. Ask the junk-food manufacturers, who are wrestling with a ban on UK TV advertising as I write. Ask Nike, Gap, Wal-Mart, *et al.*, all of whom have been condemned for using underage sweatshop workers. Ask Michael Jackson, whose standing as the premier brand in pop music plummeted almost beyond salvage in the aftermath of his alleged kiddie entanglements.

Madonna has likewise discovered the problems posed by ill-considered kiddie campaigns. Her high-profile adoption of a Malawian orphan, David Banda, proved to be a public-relations nightmare. She was accused of buying a baby on impulse as one would pick up a packet of Lifesavers at the checkout. She was condemned for attempting to circumvent proper adoption procedures in both Malawi and the UK. She should have used her celebrity, some cynics said, for the benefit of African orphans as a whole, not cherry-picking a child for egocentric, look-at-me-I'm-wonderful PR purposes.

To be sure, Madonna is well used to coping with contro-versy. Making the most of opprobrium is central to her never-ending marketing campaign. Only a few months before the Malawi kerfuffle, our shock-sells supremo was winding up the

Vatican with a crucifixion scene in her *Confessions* roadshow. But messing with children, as it were, is treacherous marketing territory. Brands have imploded over less. Sunny D, for example. It would be profoundly ironic if a brand built on shock-horror salacity were to fall into ruination over an innocent child.

Icarus may be waiting in the wings while Madge is caught in the spotlight of public disapproval, but Madonna has flown close to the sun on numerous occasions.[40] And lived to sell the tale. One of the biggest stars in the galaxy of rock, she survives and thrives in an industry where the survival rate is almost infinitesimal. Whatever else is said about her, the fact remains that she's had more hit singles than anyone bar Elvis, who died on her nineteenth birthday.

Interestingly, she saw the King's expiry as a fateful omen. It stimulated her initial attempts at emulation, despite the minor problem of having no musical know-how. A wannabe dancer, Madonna Louise Veronica Ciccone moved to New York in July 1978, where she did what was necessary to make a living on the margins of showbusiness (waitressing, scamming, hustling, hanging out, porno photosessions, counter clerk at Dunkin' Donuts). Her big break came in 1982, when she charmed Seymour Stein, the boss of Sire Records, into releasing her first single, "Everybody," which was a dance-floor sensation. "Holiday," "Burning up" and "Lucky star" soon followed, along with her bestselling eponymous album. However, it was her scandalous performance of "Like a virgin" on the 1984 *MTV Awards Show* that transported the writhing whippersnapper to the next level. Her reputation was cemented by the landmark video for "Material girl," a virtuoso pastiche of *Gentlemen Prefer Blondes*, and sealed by the furore that surrounded "Like a prayer," which achieved the remarkable double of offending both the Catholic Church and her sponsor, Pepsi Cola, while topping the charts.

Madonna kept the pot boiling with the Blonde "pointy bra"

Ambition tour, then allowed it to boil over with the wilfully explicit *Sex* book, a series of sub-par performances in quasi-porn movies, a smattering of offensive television appearances on American chat shows, and a poorly received album of uninspiring songs, *Erotica*. Undeterred, if somewhat chastened, she paused for breath, rethought her marketing strategy and bounced back with a commanding performance in *Evita*, as well as a critically acclaimed album, *Ray of Light*, and a series of I'll-show-'em singles. The Drowned World tour of 2001 confirmed her status as one of the world's top-grossing acts. Having forced her way back to the top, Madonna has not only maintained the momentum with a series of hit singles, theatrical appearances, and feature-length documentaries but reclaimed her position at the very pinnacle of her profession with a show-stopping set at Live8, the worldwide number one "Hung up," the remarkable retro album *Confessions on a Dance Floor*, a tie-in tour that broke all rock-show revenue records, and yet another knock-em-dead performance at Live Earth, Al Gore's recent eco-fest.

Musical achievements aside, Madonna is best known for her career-long role as a sexual, religious, and political provocateuse – a raunchy thorn in society's side – as well as her infinite mutability. *Femme fatale*, single parent, material girl, earth mother, hippie chick, gay icon, lesbian lover, professional virgin, sexual deviant, disco dancer, domestic goddess, spiritual spokesperson, English aristocrat, mockney geezer, Kabbalah crank, demanding diva, tough-love supermom, kid-lit author, muscle-bound hard-body, AIDS spokesperson and, if you will, Malawi's foremost procreational tourist.

What she really is, of course, is a marketing genius. If, as Germaine Greer observes, "the true art form of our time isn't music or poetry, it's marketing," then Madonna is one of the pre-eminent artists of the twenty-first century. She's the best Madgevertiser in the world today. She's blessed with a remarkable ability to keep the media spotlight trained on her every move and is acutely aware of how headlines contribute to the bottom line. She's a music-business mogul with her own record label, a production company, and diverse subsidiaries devoted to publishing, multi-media, merchandising, and similar ancillaries.[41] She's a hands-on executive who is famously frugal with her estimated personal fortune of half a billion dollars.

She is also infamously perfectionist, notoriously litigious, and an extremely tough negotiator. She maximizes her commercial potential with ads for BMW, H&M, Gap, and Motorola among others, as well as a kiddie clothing line, while taking steps to avoid overexposure in terms of available product, not ongoing PR. She has parlayed what most agree is a modest musical talent into one of the longest and most successful careers in show business, a career that shows few signs of slackening. She has, as Seymour Stein once observed, "a great sense of sell."

But what are the elements of Madge's dollar-sniffing savvy? Well, controversy is crucial. Madonna's appetite for affront is phenomenal. She is a serial controversialist, a sensationalist supreme. From her schoolyard exhibitionism, through the Pope's repeated threats to excommunicate her for blasphemy, to her onstage erotic acrobatics with the national flag of Puerto Rico, Madonna has mastered the art of scandal-mongering. Profanity, promiscuity, sacrilege, crucifixion, bisexuality, abortion, violence, terrorism, rape, child abuse, masturbation, and – arguably the most heinous crime in western culture – sharing the stage with a bagpiper are just some of the many taboos she has traded upon.

In 1990, to pick one incident among many, our Warren Buffet of the shock market engineered an MTV ban on her lesbian-kiss video "Justify my love." Thanks to the ensuing publicity, she proceeded to sell 400,000 copies of the $9.99 videotape, released just in time for the Christmas market. Ten years later, she repeated the trick with "What it feels like for a girl," a grisly video nasty directed by Guy Richie, her action-movie–obsessed significant other. This depicted the diva driving around in a souped-up auto with senior citizen in tow, indulging in all sorts of unspeakable acts, including robbery, arson, and a two-cop shoot-out. Even though her intention was satirical – she squirts the cops with a water pistol – the video was immediately outlawed, a chorus of cash registers rang in happy harmony, and another hit single was neatly notched up.

Constraint is equally central to Madge's allure. Leaving them begging for more may be a hoary showbiz cliché, but it's one that Madonna swears by. From the outset of her career she has resisted giving encores, preferring to leave audiences frustrated rather than sated. She seldom goes on the road – only six major tours in 25 years – and when she does the number of dates is strictly limited. Her sets, at 90 minutes or thereabouts, are comparatively short, though what they lack in length and longueurs they make up for in surprise, spectacle, and sheer theatricality thanks to the frequent costume changes, elaborate dance routines, and dramatic special effects.

Madonna brilliantly combines hard-to-get with over-the-top to create a hard-to-top attraction. The inevitable upshot of this HTT strategy is that her shows are instant sell-outs, which dramatically reduces associated promotional expenditure; her ticket prices are premium-plus, the highest in the industry by far; and her tours are extremely profitable despite the enormous staging costs. Indeed, it has been estimated that the 60-date *Confessions* tour grossed a record $195 million worldwide. When you consider that touring has long been regarded as a loss leader for money-spinning albums, Madonna's profit-centred approach is no mean achievement and as hard-nosed as they come.

A third crucial element is contrariety. Madonna goes against the grain. She's a subversive at heart – her penchant for underwear as outerwear says it all – and nowhere more so than in her attitude to consumers. Whatever else it is, Madonna marketing is most definitely not predicated on customer coddling. On the contrary, our diva deluxe treats her audience abominably and they love her for it. She attracts customers by refusing to pander to them, by tantalizing, tormenting, and teasing them, by playing hard to get, by making them work for it, beg for it, abase themselves before her.

Madge's stage persona during 2001's *Drowned World* tour, for example, was profane and contemptuous by turns. Her inter-song patter eschewed love y'all showbiz platitudes for "Fuck you, motherfuckers" and analogous customer-isn't-king marketing epigrams. With the exception of "Holiday," she refused to play any of her greatest hits, preferring to focus on less audience-friendly material. The show ended not with hot-rockin', hand-wavin', lighter-holdin' encores or hard-earned curtain calls but with a video clip on a giant screen informing the audience that "She ain't comin' back, so go on, piss off." Bearing in mind that the tour was her first in nine years, a period when her career sank to its lowest commercial ebb, Madonna's "forget the customer" stance was bold, brazen, ballsy, and, above all, deliciously, seditiously contrarian. Sell it like it is, Ciccone!

STEVE JOBS (1955–)
There is an "I" in Apple

There's an oft-recounted anecdote that tells you everything you need to know about Steve Jobs. While working part-time for Atari, the company behind Pong, Gran Trak, and many other classic arcade games, Steve was asked to help with an R&D project. If he could iron the kinks out of a demo game called *Breakout*, there'd be a bunch of extra bucks for him. So young Jobs got his best buddy, computer whiz Steve Wozniak, to do the grunt work – *all* the grunt work, since his own programming skills were negligible – and received $1,000 for his efforts.

Naturally, he split the money with Woz, the future co-founder of Apple Computers. It wasn't a 50/50 split, however. Steve told Woz he'd received $600 for *Breakout* and generously split that 50/50 with his giga-brained sidekick. As far as Jobs was concerned, 70/30 seemed fair and what Woz didn't know wouldn't do him any harm. Woz found out a few years later, to his understandable dismay, but by that stage the scales had fallen from his eyes about the one and only Jobster.[42]

The Applemeister's ability to sell a bill of goods to his partner wasn't just a youthful peccadillo. On the contrary, Steve Jobs' biographers allege that he has repeatedly reneged on deals and double-crossed those around him. Loveable he ain't. At the time of Apple's early-eighties ascendancy, he allegedly persuaded a supplier to sink millions into a bespoke processor that'd power the next generation of machines. Then he abruptly changed his mind, welshed on the deal, and left VLSI without a silicon leg to stand on. Several years later, after the Apple putsch of 1985 in which our cuddly IT titan was unceremoniously canned, and then turned his hand to the animated movie business, a leading computer company took an interest in Pixar's RenderMan software. Reportedly, they negotiated for months, a lucrative deal was done, much executive time and energy was expended, then Steve had second thoughts and told them to swivel on it. They swivelled. Jobs didn't give a shit.

Nor indeed did he give a shit (allegedly) when it came to engineering the 1995 ouster of Apple chairperson Gil Amelio, the man who'd done much to turn the company around after its early 1990s collapse under former Pepsi supremo John Sculley. Gil had not only bought NeXT, the high-end computer company that Jobs founded during his period of post-Apple perdition, but also brought Steve back into the Apple fold as interim CEO. Our hero allegedly stabbed Amelio in the back and took the credit for his achievements. Gil had been responsible for the restructuring that put Apple on the road to profitability. Steve benefited accordingly and received all the PR plaudits.

Jobs clearly doesn't have much time for "customers," be they suppliers, investors, distributors, or even employees. At the Apple IPO of 1980, he denied share options to the people who were working 90-hour weeks to get his products to market. He treated Pixar employees the same way when it too was floated in the immediate aftermath of *Toy Story*'s triumph. He is notorious for his kick-ass, in-your-face, who-the-fuck-are-you-and-what-makes-you-worth-what-I-pay-you management style, which hardly qualifies as textbook touchy-feely, happy-clappy, no-I-in-team best practice. What else do you expect from the only son of a repo man?

Actually, Steve doesn't think much of the end user either. From the Mac to the iPod, he has consistently refused to make Apple's software compatible with alternative operating systems, even though it'd make consumers' lives a lot easier. He also appreciates the power of strategic shortages – the strictly limited availability of the first iPhones, for example – which drove gotta-have-it devotees certifiably crazy, such was their desire to get their hands on the elusive exclusive product.

Customer coddling may not be part of Steve Jobs' job description, but he possesses a personal quality of paramount importance in business life, one that is well represented among our Fail Incredibly Betters: ruthlessness. Granted, the Apple icon isn't as brutal as Gabriele d'Annunzio, whose savagery on the page extended to real life too. Nor, come to think of it, is Steve as nasty as Coco Chanel, who took advantage of Nazi-imposed wartime legislation to disinherit her Jewish business partners. All things considered, though, Steve scores approximately eight out of ten on the Hannibal Lecter-ometer. Indeed, if playing hardball with stakeholders is one of the keys to commercial success, as Michael O'Leary, Rupert Murdoch, Madonna, and legions of bellicose management consultants indicate, then Steve Jobs must be blessed with the hardest balls in California.

None of the stories surrounding Steven Paul Jobs – his aggression, his arrogance, his assholeosity, his alleged transgressions over backdated share options – should detract from his marketing genius. Salesmen don't come any better. Nor indeed more precocious. Brought up by foster parents in Cupertino, California, Steve showed his sales prowess at an early age. He sweet-talked Bill Hewlett, of Hewlett-Packard fame, into giving him free parts for a high-school project and extracted valuable components from computer giant Burroughs by intimating that his "company" was evaluating potential suppliers. His schoolteacher was appalled by this behaviour, not least because Jobs called Burroughs collect. Similarly, he strong-armed his penurious parents into sending him to an expensive liberal arts college in Oregon and then repaid them by dropping out, dropping drugs, and disappearing off on the hippie trail to find himself. What he discovered, presumably, was the huckster within.

On his return from India, Jobs hooked up with old pal Steve Wozniak, who'd previously helped the IT trickster sell his illegal "blue boxes," a Skype-style telephony finagle that gave the owners free calls. More important, he convinced the Woz that there was a business in his circuit boards and that their company should be called Apple rather than something unspeakably nerdish. When Apple I hit the streets in 1976, furthermore, it was Jobs who hustled it into reluctant computer stores; when the Apple II revolutionized personal computing in 1977, it was Jobs who masterminded the knock-em-dead launch at Expo 77 and promptly became the poster boy for the suddenly sexy Silicon Valley brigade.

More fundamentally, it was Jobs who saw the future during that famously fateful visit to Xerox's PARC facility in 1979, when the possibilities inherent in GUI (graphical user interface), object-oriented software, pull-down menus, and a funny pointing device with two buttons called a mouse struck him like a Pentium-powered thunderbolt. Jobs too was the driving force behind the iconic Macintosh, which made its unforgettable debut during the 1984 Superbowl. At a time when the company was so strapped for cash that its board attempted to cancel the advertising slot it had purchased at enormous expense, Steve supported the showing of "1984," the landmark television commercial that was broadcast only once yet ranks among the most effective TV ads of all time.[43]

Jobs' chutzpah may make Donald Trump look like a shrinking violet, Sam Walton a bedwetting wimp, and Aimee Semple McPherson a tongue-tied anchorite, but he shares The Donald's visionary ability. Whatever his character flaws, immodesty issues, and interpersonal skills shortcomings, Steve's ability to sell spellbinding visions of the future is unsurpassed, nay unsurpassable. Even his sternest critics, his sworn enemies, and the sadder-but-wiser victims of his psychic punishment beatings acknowledge that his sales-pitch prowess is phenomenal. He's the kinda guy who could not only sell ice to Inuits but get them to buy a refrigerator to store the freakin' frozen stuff.

He has a slogan for every occasion – "Insanely great,"

"Think different," "Real artists ship," "The journey is the reward," "Let's make a dent in the universe" – and his annual presentations at the Macworld Expo are nothing less than works of performance art. As a biographer says about one particular make-or-break sales pitch delivered at the absolute nadir of Jobs' career, "He speaks with the fluency of someone in total command of his subject, the passion of someone totally committed, and exactly the right control over his listeners' emotions. It's a remarkable performance, so convincing that you could listen for an hour without interrupting, so compelling that you wonder whether he might not have had an amazingly successful career as another Jack Nicholson or Jeff Bridges."[44]

In keeping with the Fail Better trajectory, furthermore, Steve Jobs has experienced more ups and downs than a crackhead on antidepressants. For every IT triumph – Apple II, Macintosh, iMac, iPod, iTunes – he has had a calamitous failure. Lisa, Apple III, NeXT Workstation, and the G4 cube are just some of the many mistakes that Steven Paul Jobs has presided over. He was unceremoniously cashiered from the company he created by the very person he appointed CEO, John Sculley. He spent ten years in the hero-to-zero wilderness and almost lost everything during his nest-egg-gobbling adventures with NeXT and Pixar, only to return as conquering hero. He has enjoyed a stunning run of post-return successes, the iPod family in particular, but as the market for MP3 players matures some very risky decisions lie ahead …

Will downloadable movies take off? How will competitors respond to the iPhone? Are Apple-brand plasma-screen TVs and similar Sony-style appliances a possibility? Is the recent move to Windows-compatible Intel processors a potential killer app or the beginning of the Apple end? Can Microsoft come up with a counterblow – an iPod crusher, a Tiger hit squad, a visionary Vista alternative? When will Pixar's run of hit movies end? (*Cars* definitely put the brakes on.) Now that it's Disney's baby and Steve is the biggest shareholder in the Magic Kingdom, will Mickey's mouse be incompatible with Apple software? Who can say, but don't bet against Jobs selling his way out of trouble.

VIJAY MALLYA (1955–)

The Future is Now

India is the new America. Rapid economic growth, abundant natural resources, a well-educated workforce with easy proficiency in English, impressively irrepressible entrepreneurial flair, and above all the surging self-confidence of a country on the up all suggest that the future is orange, white, and green.[45]

Indeed, if the emerging cadre of Indian businesspeople is anything to go by, hitherto unassailable American capitalism is in for a Lola Montez–style thrashing. Mukesh and Anil Ambani, the warring brothers of the diversified Reliance Group; Ratan Tata, the trucks-to-teabags empire builder; Sunil Bharti Mittal, the maharaja of mobile phones who aspires to supermarket suzerainty; Samir and Vineet Jain, monster media moguls (think Rupees Murdoch); Rita Kumar, the Coco Chanel of Delhi-chic, little black saris a speciality; Nadan Nilekani, the king of outsourcing who advocates outsourcing outsourcing to places like, um, Ulster ... I could go on. With 20 million people entering the workforce annually and ever-increasing direct foreign investment, future waves of Indiannovation are inevitable. Six hundred years ago, Columbus was looking for India and found America. Maybe he should have kept going.

Vijay Mallya exemplifies New India. Larger than larger than life, he is endowed with a $1 billion fortune, ranks 28th on India's rich list, and is renowned for his fast cars, fast horses, and faster-than-fast lifestyle.[46] He owns palatial homes in copious cosmopolitan cities including London, Paris, and San Francisco. He drips with corporate jets, yachts, helicopters, and similar big-business baubles. He is medallion man Mumbai-style, shackled in solid-gold jewellery, chunky diamond earrings, and sufficient designer shades to put Bono to shame.

Actually, if you can imagine a cross between Bono and Donald Trump, only more ostentatious, you begin to get the picture.

As you might expect, Mallya throws lavish parties, collects vintage cars, consorts with Sting, Lionel Richie, and analogous nabobs of rock royalty, plays an enormous kick-ass drumkit in his spare time, owns a modest miscellany of modern art masterpieces by Picasso, Renoir, Chagall, *et al.*, and, it almost goes without saying, keeps a pad on permanent standby in Trump Tower, New York. In keeping, furthermore, with our big-hair hypothesis, he dyes his beard, highlights his locks, and for all I know wears a chest wig. On formal occasions, Mallya's bouffant hairdo looks not unlike a hirsute Taj Mahal, complete with cupolas and minarets. I kid you not.

Many have dismissed Vijay Mallya as a frivolous playboy, an entrepreneurial airhead with more money than sense, a fratboy fatcat hell-bent on squandering his father's stupendous legacy. Vijay, it's true, didn't build his business from scratch. The eldest son of Vittal Mallya, an Indian beer baron, he was born with a silver tankard in his admittedly big mouth. Based in Bangalore, the United Beverages Group was founded by Scotsman Thomas Leishman in 1857 and largely dedicated to slaking the thirst of off-duty British soldiers. It fell into Vittal's lap in the aftermath of independence, when prohibition was briefly mooted, and with phenomenal flair and drive he initiated a programme of acquisitions in the 1950s and 1960s, expanded the UB portfolio into wines and spirits, and eventually diversified into agribusiness, petrochemicals, pharmaceuticals, and infrastructure construction.

The company devolved to Vijay on his father's death in 1983. As a 27-year-old going on 17, the UB legatee "lived his age" – read "went wild and crazy" – for a few unforgettable years that he'd rather not remember. He became a media baron, bought a daily paper, dabbled in film-making, ran a stable of glossy magazines, started a software firm in the States, bought a couple of US breweries, and acquired a Napa Valley vineyard or two. As one does when a breathtaking bequest is burning a hole in one's Armani pocket.

Nowadays, Mallya claims to be the uncrowned King of Good Times. With some justification. He genuinely believes that impoverished Indians admire his extravagant lifestyle and consider him a twenty-first-century role model. He even has the gall to call himself a son of the soil. The rationale for this tongue-in-cheek claim is that he once crashed his private helicopter in a field somewhere in the sticks, and not only lived to tell the tale but wove the yarn into a self-serving myth about horny-handedness, getting in touch with Mother India, etc. Brass neck, steel balls, silver tongue, tungsten sixpack, call it what you will.

At the same time, Mallya has built United Breweries into India's biggest beverage conglomerate, with 52 percent of the beer market (up from 18 percent in 1983) and approximately 60 percent of the wines and spirits sector. His Kingfisher brand is the bestselling beer in India with a quarter share of the market, and is available in 32 countries worldwide. A series of judicious acquisitions, most notably the Scottish distiller Whyte & Mackay, the French winemaker Bouvet-Ladubay, and long-term rival Indian brewer Shaw Wallace, have established UB as the dominant player in the industry and the second-biggest liquor company in the world after Diageo. What's more, having reorganized the group by divesting companies bought in haste, consolidating the unwieldy empire into coherent operating divisions, and making astute investments in high-return enterprises (as with the sizeable stake in pharmaceuticals giant Aventis), Mallya is much more than a mere playboy of the eastern world, or the star-struck purchaser of a yacht previously owned by Elizabeth Taylor, or the puffed-up possessor of the legendary sword of Tipu, once the property of the Sultan of Mysore and latterly lent to the Indian nation as a symbol of the country's remarkable renaissance.

Mallya, above all, is a brand-builder *par excellence*. Banned from advertising alcoholic beverages, he still managed to build Kingfisher into India's best-known brand. Surveys show that its logo is one of the most recognized on the subcontinent, bigger even than McDonald's or Microsoft. This towering marketing achievement was attained by advertising *in absentia*. Events sponsorship, clothing lines, fashion awards, ownership of racehorses, racing cars, football teams *et al.*, and his own high-profile exploits – not least his election as an MP in India's upper house of parliament – have ensured that the Kingfisher logo is plastered everywhere that matters. The Kingfisher Derby, for instance, is held every year in the burgeoning city of Bangalore and represents the highlight of the conurbation's social calendar. Like Sir Thomas Lipton, moreover, Vijay is conscious that a sense of corporate social responsibility is especially incumbent on sellers of fast-moving consumer goods – the more frequent the contact, the more fragile the brand image – and has established the Mallya Hospital, the Mallya Aditi International School, and the Vittal Mallya Research Foundation, among others.

It is little wonder, then, that Mallya is known as The Boss. He is also known as the Richard Branson of India, if only because his most recent ruse is Kingfisher Airlines. Initially laughed off as a dilettantish dabbler, Mallya has seized the opportunity afforded by Indian airline deregulation to build up an impressive network of intercity routes. Funky, fun-loving, full-service, fashion-forward, frill-filled, and furnished with a fleet of brand new Airbus A330s, A350s, and even a couple of A380s on order, Kingfisher Airlines has been an instant success. Its world-class entertainment system, three-course gourmet meals, and high-heeled, tight-skirted, all-female cabin crew have done much to put Kingfisher Airlines on the map, if not elevating it to a bastion of equal opportunities. Its unreconstructed ethos, vaguely reminiscent (for those of you with long memories) of Caledonian Girls, hasn't stopped Kingfisher collecting numerous industry awards including Best New Airline in 2005. International routes are also high on the agenda, as is the repeal of the domestic ban on in-flight alcoholic beverages. Kingfisher beer will surely be the first thirst-quenching brew available to New India's airborne billions.

Though often made, the Branson comparison is rather unfair on Mallya. Vijay is a much better marketer than Branson, especially in light of the political and legislative impediments he's faced. Whereas Branson always gives the impression that his heart isn't in the Virgin showmanship – a contrived air permeates every publicity stunt, and the rictus grin doesn't help either – Vijay Mallya is a natural. Or, to be more precise, he's a better actor than Branson. Like Morita, Trump, and O'Leary, Mallya puts his all into the role. The brand and the man are indistinguishable. Richard Branson, for all his admirable marketing achievements, is an enthusiastic amateur by comparison. Mallya is Royal Shakespeare Company to his student dramsoc. Bearing in mind the regulatory hurdles he's overcome and the cultural context from whence he hails, Vijay Mallya is the heir to P. T. Barnum and a harbinger of the future of marketing management.

P. T. BARNUM (1810–91)
This Way to the Egress

Not a lot of people know this, but P. T. Barnum was one of the world's first management consultants. Seventy years before McKinsey coined the phrase and Marvin Bower cut his consulting milk teeth, the peerless Phineas Taylor Barnum was disbursing advice on business matters.[47] It is somehow appropriate and singularly ironic, I'm sure you'll agree, that management consultancy was invented by the man who said "There's a sucker born every minute." It is doubly appropriate and spookily ironic that the reason he got into the advice-giving business was because of a watch and clock company that went bankrupt, dragged Barnum down with it and forcing him to tramp the public-speaking circuit in order to replay his ruinous debts.

Prior to the 1856 collapse of the Jerome Clock Company, P. T. Barnum was one of the richest men in America and by far the most famous showman in the world. From his rock-bottom start running a grocery store (it failed), editing a newspaper (it tanked), hawking lottery tickets (unsuccessfully) and, I kid you not, selling better mousetraps (albeit few customers beat a path to his door), he found his metier in the world of showmanship. Curiosities were his speciality, oddities his commodities, what-is-it wonders his stock-in-trade. Human, semi-human, or otherwise, all were grist to Barnum's marketing mill.

He made his name with Joice Heth, the supposedly 161-year-old slave who had attended George Washington's birth and told such fantastic stories about nursing the Father of the Country that punters couldn't get enough of her. Until she died, of course, and an autopsy revealed she was 80 years old, max. She was a fake, in other words, an imposture, a humbug, the first of many from Barnum, the self-styled Prince of Humbugs.

Heth wasn't long in her grave when the superlative

showman rolled out his "mermaid from Fijee." Attracted by come-hither posters of a fish-tailed hottie – think *Splash*, only sexier – crowds flocked to see this piscine apparition, only to be confronted with a hideous tribute to creative taxidermy: half baboon, half barracuda, all Barnum. The real beauty, however, was that you couldn't see the join, and when attendance started to slacken, the great showman sold the spectacle for a second time on the compelling platform "Fake or real? You decide!"

Fresh from his aquatic triumph, the peerless PT struck gold with his greatest pre-collapse hit, a 25-inch midget called Charles S. Stratton. Barnum renamed him General Tom Thumb, taught him a quick-fire stage routine, dressed him in miniature uniforms – Napoleon, Caesar, etc. – and toured the tiny titan throughout the civilized world to enormous acclaim and untold riches. The crowned heads of Europe, Queen Victoria in particular, were enchanted with the little man and Barnum used their patronage to excellent marketing effect. Celebrity endorsement didn't get much better, and Barnum wasn't one to hide his promotional light under a monarchical bushel. Royalties doesn't begin to describe it.

Inevitably Icarus wrapped his wax wings around the arrogant young showman. A soaraway success he may have been, but vaunting vanity begets hubris and hubris calls up nemesis. In his 1854 autobiography *The Life of P. T. Barnum, Written By Himself*, the author boasted of his hoaxes, hooplas, and humbugs. Genteel society was infuriated, not merely by the outrageous impostures but by the fact that the conman revelled in his customer-gulling contrivances.[48]

But Barnum didn't care. All publicity was good publicity. His book outsold everything bar the Bible. He could do no wrong. He had the magic touch. He was the greatest marketer in America, with millions in the bank. He owned an enormous mansion, Iranistan, modelled on the Brighton Pavilion only less understated. He ran the biggest tourist attraction in New York City, the must-see American Museum on Broadway. His name was on everyone's lips thanks to a string of high-profile pranks from a supposedly woolly horse to an incredible free buffalo hunt in Hoboken, New Jersey, and he'd written a swaggering autobiography of such staggering vainglory that Donald Trump's recent efforts seem self-effacing by comparison.[49]

Like his latter-day gilded avatar, moreover, P. T. Barnum was a master property developer as well as a canny investor in numerous up-and-coming companies. Until he wound up with the Jerome Clock Company. Regarded as an employment magnet for his residential property developments in East Bridgeport, Jerome couldn't be allowed to fail. So Barnum sank vast sums into the clockwork goose that was going to lay the golden egg. But the only egg was on the showman's face, as it happens, and few had much sympathy for the bankrupt blowhard.

Failure, appropriately, was the making of Barnum. Drawing on his business experience, both good and bad, the Prince of Humbugs concocted a how-to package called "The Art of Money Getting." A more apt tile, he joked, would be "The Art of Money Losing," but his "Art" offer proved enormously successful. He went on the stump. Night after night after night, he filled fly-blown halls in jerry-built towns with wannabe millionaires. He told them how to make a fortune. Unlike his worthy but dull competitors on the Lyceum circuit, he retailed an attractive combination of sage advice, funny stories, arresting visual aids – the Fijee mermaid in the flesh! – and occasional magic-cum-juggling tricks. A wonderful amalgam of Billy Connolly, Tommy Cooper, Steven Covey, and The Donald, P. T. Barnum's management roadshow was a barnstormer and a half. It couldn't fail. It didn't. So successful was his Art of Money Getting operation (complete with tie-in book, the infamous autobiography) that he paid off all his debts in double-quick time.

By 1860, he was back in harness at the ripe old age of 50. His greatest triumphs, the ones he's still remembered for, lay ahead of him. Chastened by abject failure, he built a better future. Reinvented decades before Disney as "the children's friend" and regarded as the quintessential Yankee pedlar, Barnum attained his apotheosis with The Greatest Show on Earth, an experiential extravaganza that remains unsurpassed in the annals of showbusiness. An amalgam of Mardi Gras, stadium rock, Olympics opening ceremony and Cirque du Soleil on steroids, The Greatest Show on Earth was a fitting tribute to the ultimate exponent of Fail Better practice.

Be that as it may, the really interesting thing about P. T. Barnum's Art of Money Getting roadshow is that it is just as relevant today as it was 150 years ago. If we overlook the unfortunate sprinkling of Irish jokes – a shameful act of cultural stereotyping, if I say so myself – Barnum's programme still has much to offer. It identifies the causes of failure in business, preaches the benefits of fail-better learning experiences, advocates an indomitable never-say-die attitude, and sets out his rules for removing failure's icy fingers from the wannabe's windpipe. These formulations include precursors of Tom Peters' "stick to your knitting" ("Do not scatter your powers"), Jim Collins' "big hairy audacious goals" ("Let hope predominate"), Ben and Jerry's corporate responsibility ("Be charitable"), and, incredibly, Danny Miller's Icarus hypothesis ("Don't get above your business").

Nevertheless, the single biggest item on Barnum's how-to checklist, the rule he devoted most attention to, concerned marketing. "Advertise your business," he advocated. Then advertise it again and again and again. It's impossible, so Barnum believed, to advertise too much. Cheeseparing on advertising is the biggest mistake a businessperson can make. The object is to make people aware of what you're selling. While the actual product or service must be acceptable – ideally outstanding – the failure to familiarize people about its availability is a recipe for disaster.

These were sensible sentiments in 1858. They are equally wise words today. Barnum wasn't called the Shakespeare of advertising for nothing. Just as *Hamlet* speaks to successive generations of readers, so too Barnum's *Struggles and*

Triumphs is more insightful than any number of much-hyped management bestsellers, *Fail Better!* excepted.

Space does not permit a detailed discussion of P. T. Barnum's marketing achievements. A multi-volume anthology is the minimum needed to do the Prince of Humbugs justice. However, there is one Barnumarketing talent that is well worth noting. He understood the power of denial, withdrawal, subtraction, lack. He appreciated that removing something of value, even the most taken-for-granted possession, is a behavioural stimulus like no other. Making things unobtainable, especially if they were previously freely available, is a much better way of getting a reaction than any amount of get-a-load-of-this persuasion.

When he engineered the acquisition of Jumbo, a giant African elephant, from London Zoo in 1881, he precipitated a national outcry, an incidence of agonized hand-wringing that wasn't attained again until Duveen recapitulated Barnum's stunt with *The Blue Boy*. Indeed, its mutant descendants stalk marketing to this day. Lack underpinned the New Coke debacle in 1987. Lack is responsible for the appeal of banned movies and books (the *Lady Chatterley* effect) or extra-exclusive, almost unobtainable fashion items (the Birkin bag effect). Lack motivates the fury many people feel when supermarkets rearrange their merchandise without warning, or brand consultancies come up with the bright idea of renaming much-loved consumables like Marathon or Opal Fruits, or when providers of utilities such as gas, water, electricity, phone lines, and internet connections leave their customers in the lurch, or when swingeing branch closures are announced by, say, Barclays Bank or the Post Office.

The difference, of course, is that Barnum knew how to handle this ever-powerful proprietorial emotion and turn it to his best promotional advantage. And what, I hear you ask, is the secret of denial marketing?

Drat, my word limit is up ...

★ 4 ★

WHO'S THE DADDY?

An indigent author writes a compelling story about an eleven-year-old orphan with wayward hair and distinctive features who is transported to another place, finds it difficult to fit in and, after getting into all sorts of intriguing scrapes, eventually learns to do the right thing. The manuscript of the story is rejected by numerous publishing houses that see no market for the quirky tale. Our author is on the point of giving up and returning to her hardscrabble job as a teacher, but on a whim decides to try one last publisher. The manuscript is accepted and published in a limited edition, and miraculously becomes an enormous hit. The formerly indigent author follows up with sequel after sequel, and a storybook franchise is born.

Familiar as it is, this rags-to-riches tale of literary good fortune is not the heart-warming story of J. K. Rowling and the Harry Potter phenomenon. It is the tale of L. M. Montgomery, an impecunious inhabitant of Price Edward Island whose classic children's story *Anne of Green Gables* was published in 1908 to huge popularity, instant acclaim, and no little criticism. It is a story that spawned six successful sequels, all of which have been filmed, televised, merchandised, and variously recycled in the century since *Anne of Green Gables* was written.[1]

Montgomery's story, nevertheless, is almost identical to Jo Rowling's, even down to the six sequels. JKR published her first Harry Potter novel in 1997 and saw her creation grow and grow and grow as episode after episode rolled off the Rowling production line. Still, it just goes to show that there's nothing new in marketing. We like to think that our times are more competitive, more challenging, more changeable than they were way back when. Not so. Competition has always been tough, unforgiving, and subject to sudden waves of innovation that sweep the old order away. Failure rates were just as fierce 50 years ago as they are today. If anything, they were fiercer back then because our era is one of unusual abundance and economic prosperity.

Today's breakthrough marketing ideas – buzz marketing, guerrilla marketing, neuromarketing, permission marketing – are no more than old ideas reconfigured, repackaged, resold. Even retromarketing, our current preoccupation with times past, isn't new. Nostalgia was big back in the 1970s, 1930s, and 1890s, and no doubt today's revivals will be revived in the fullness of time.[2] Who knows for sure? Prediction isn't exactly marketing's strong point, cool hunting, trend spotting, and scenario planning notwithstanding. All we can say for certain is that future marketers will be faced with extremely difficult challenges, just like their manifold predecessors.

Consider the predicament confronting James Patterson one hundred years ago. He sold the latest B2B technology, the cash register. This was an innovation that retailers didn't want or need because they'd been doing business perfectly well without it for centuries. The cash register was a very expensive machine, what's more, and traders then as now weren't exactly renowned for their extravagance, especially when it came to splashing out on unnecessary technology. Shop assistants, similarly, were totally opposed to the new device, which not only impugned their honesty but was certain to put many of them out of work. There was no shortage of competitors either

– competitors who weren't reluctant to badmouth their rivals, sabotage their machines, or plant fifth columnists in order to undermine morale and uncover trade secrets. Patterson's company, National Cash Register, also had the aftermarket to contend with: dealers in secondhand or refurbished registers that did the job just as well as NCR's spanking new machines for a lot less money.

Yet Patterson turned NCR into a commercial powerhouse, the foremost marketing organization of its time. His sales-training programmes were superb. He built the best salesforce in the world and developed a sales manual that covered every angle, every objection, every obstacle, every barrier to doing business. Predicated on the hard-sell tactics of itinerant evangelists, religious revivalists, and buy-one-or-go-to-Hell Bible salespersons, NCR was a secular version of the Salvation Army. It had a salesforce whose methods were embraced by – to name but three – Charles Kettering of General Motors, Thomas Watson of IBM, and William Benton of the Benton & Bowles advertising agency, none of whom were slouches in the selling department.

My point, then, is that rather than focus on the latest marketing campaign, cool brand, dot.com sensation, or even best-selling how-to book, we can turn to the past for inspiration. We can learn just as much, or maybe more, from Marvin Bower or Edward Bernays than Tom Peters or Jim Collins. Likewise, we can look outside the business and management community, since the most creative marketers don't necessarily work for GE or P&G or Coca-Cola or even Innocent Drinks, nor do they necessarily possess me-too MBAs from prestigious universities. Creative artists like Madonna or Jeff Koons or J. K. Rowling are more marketing-savvy than serried ranks of Harvard or Wharton or Northwestern MBAs. The markets Koons and co. compete in, what's more, are just as tough if not tougher than those faced by B-school educated replicants, simulants, Ps in a pod.

But is Madonna a better marketer than Lola Montez? Certainly not. Is Rupert Murdoch more ruthless or calculating than Coco Chanel? Tough call. Is The Donald's monstrous ego a patch on that possessed by Italian stallion Gabriele d'Annunzio? I don't think so. Is the cult of Steve Jobs in the same league as the fanatical following of Anton Mesmer, Anna Held, or Aimee Semple McPherson? Nope, nope, and thrice nope. Is Sam Walton, impressive though he was in his pomp and powerful as his organization still is, really fit to swab the decks of the good ship Sir Thomas Lipton? Do I really have to answer that?

Who, in other words, is the best of the best? Best of the worst, rather? Ron Popeil? André Citroën? Akio Morita? Joseph Duveen? Before I answer that, it's necessary to reflect for a few moments on the best of the rest of the worst. As noted in chapter 3, our Fail Incredibly Betters (FIBs) were selected by a highly sophisticated process involving rigorous statistical analysis and careful calibration for culturally determined conditions past and present. Many were called, but few were chosen. Here's some of those that just missed the cut:

★ Eddie Gilbert was a supersalesperson of the late 1950s and early 1960s who expanded his lumber business into a takeover vehicle and played the stock market like a penny whistle. Even when the Boy Wonder of Wall Street was jailed for insider dealing, he managed to corner the market for cigarettes in Sing-Sing, which is some achievement. He made not one, not two, but three multi-million dollar fortunes, all from nothing. He even talked his way to a mini-fortune while on the lam in Brazil. Sadly this didn't involve selling coffee to the locals, though if anyone could've done it, it's gotta be Gilbert.

★ Roustam Tariko is the Boy Wonder of Nevsky Prospekt, the embodiment of new Russia's rags-to-rubles fantasy. He's a regular Horatio Algerovich, small-town boy made good. Born in Tartarstan and abandoned by his father, he ran off to Moscow where he started as a street cleaner saving every kopek that came his way. He seized his moment when communism went west and started importing luxuries like Smirnoff, Johnnie Walker, and ambassador's favourite Ferrero Rocher. Inspired by Smirnoff, he reinvented Russian vodka and launched a native brand in 1998. Russian Standard rapidly took off, as did his next venture, a bank specializing in consumer finance. Russian Standard is setting the standard. Watch this space.

★ Antoni Gaudí was a Catalan architect of such breathtaking arrogance that he considered Michelangelo a bumbling amateur and made Salvador Dalí look shy and retiring. He not only ignored clients' wishes while spending their money with the abandon of Imelda Marcos at Manolo's midwinter sale, but he rode roughshod over town planners, city officials, fellow architects, and the Roman Catholic Church, which is no pushover. But boy, could he sell a vision of architectural possibilities – as Casa Milà, Casa Batlló, and Sagrada Famila attest – and boy, could be turn those brilliantly sold visions into hallucinogenic reality.

★ Madam C. J. Walker was an African-American entrepreneur who overcame poverty, parental abandonment, physical abuse, misogyny, and racial discrimination. She also contended with competition in the cosmetics industry that was fierce, ferocious, and stiffer than the Botoxed incumbents of Forest Hills' celebrity cemetery. However, her hair-products company cleaned up in the early twentieth century. She established a door-to-door selling system that predated Avon and Mary Kay by decades. By 1917, she employed 3,000 agents and had become the first self-made female millionaire in the USA. Oprah had it easy by comparison.

★ Al Capone is widely regarded as the malevolent model for Jimmy Cagney's "Top of the world, ma" histrionics in *White Heat*. Actually, he was nothing like that. Tall, dark, and handsome in a scarfaced, syphilitic, muscle-running-to-fat manner, Capone was smart, sophisticated, beautifully dressed, wonderfully avuncular, and much loved by all except his sworn enemies. True, he was prone to clubbing traitorous employees' crania with baseball bats, but he was a brilliant businessman who systematized the often chaotic conditions in the Chicago bootlegging industry and marketed his brand name with Trump-like aplomb. When Capone said "You're fired," he wasn't joking.

★ Niccolò Paganini was the prototype pop star. A virtuoso violinist, he pretty much invented showmanship as we understand it. His stagecraft was second to none. He played upside down, on one string, with breathtaking glissandos, and produced musical sounds the like of which had never been heard before. He was Jimi Hendrix, Elvis Presley, James Brown, and The Beatles all rolled into one. He limped on stage pale, dishevelled, emaciated – having sold his soul to the Devil, it was rumoured – then delivered a demonic set that sent concert-goers into raptures. His ticket prices were four or five times the norm. He played charity gigs. He fought musical duels with rival violinists. He opened a casino. He went crazy. He died young.

★ Generals are not renowned for their reticence, let alone low self-esteem. Caesar, Napoleon, Patton, Montgomery: egomaniacs one and all. However, when it comes to relentless self-glorification, none can compare to General Douglas MacArthur. Undeniably brave and an astute strategist, especially in the Pacific theatre during the Second World War, his military career was never less than sensational. Top of his class at West Point, the youngest division commander in the US army, he posed for posterity and surrounded himself with a coterie of journalists and photographers who publicized his every word, most of which were "I," "me," and "mine." With his cap consistently set at a photogenically jaunty angle, he took full credit for his victories, blamed his defeats on incompetent others and unceasingly stoked the myth that he was the greatest soldier of all time. Then he made a mess of Korea and was unceremoniously sacked by President Truman. Field Marshal Failure wins again.

So, who's the best? The best of the worst? Well, my heart says P. T. Barnum, but my head says someone else. This someone else is personally responsible for perhaps the foremost marketing event in the calendar. His sales volumes are to die for. His JIT logistics are state of the art, infinitely better than Wal-Mart's. His word of mouth is so good it hurts, his personal advertising expenditure is minimal, he has strategic alliances with A-list companies, and he is an expert in outsourcing everything except the brand. His CRM systems are beyond belief: he knows all of his countless customers intimately. His CSR is second to none, something that all organizations should aspire to. He understands the importance of maintaining mystery, avoiding overexposure, heightening anticipation, and doling out free gifts à la Duveen. He operates in every sector of the economy, though toys, games, food, jewellery, apparel, books, music, DVDs, alcoholic beverages, and party planning predominate.

He is the biggest brand in the world: bigger than Coke, bigger than Disney, bigger than McDonald's. Naturally, he doesn't coddle his customers, because he expects something valuable in return and is ruthless if the deal is reneged on. He doesn't always give customers what they want, though few complain afterwards. He's been condemned by do-gooders, killjoys, and those with a regrettably rationalist mindset. He's old-fashioned and stuck in his ways; he has no truck with strategic planning, situation analyses, or fancy marketing folderol. His name never appears in the latest how-to me-too management textbooks. He remains, nonetheless, the greatest marketer who ever lived. Variously known as Santa Claus, Saint Nicholas, and Kris Kringle, Father Christmas is the guru I'm referring to.[3] *He's* the daddy!

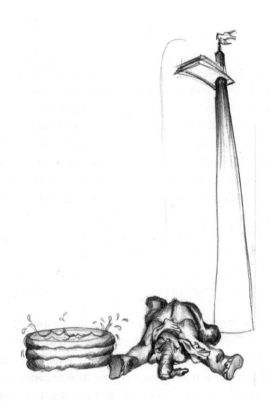

★ 5 ★

PLAYING HOPSCOTCH IN THE MARKETING MINEFIELD

When Thomas J. Watson Sr passed away in 1956, the *New York Times* described him as the world's greatest salesman. Although he wasn't the first to receive the ultimate accolade, nor indeed the last, Watson's right up there with the greats.[1] The founder of IBM not only marketed the machine that epitomizes today's hard-drive-driven society – albeit bulky first-generation versions – but he also embodies Fail Better marketing. True, the world's greatest salesman is nowadays remembered for his infamous prediction that the total all-time market for computers would be five. Yes, five. However, his life story distils the essence of our Fail Better argument and helps us extract some general lessons about marketing best practice.

Big Blue's Big Boss

Thomas J. Watson's father was a farmer of Scotch-Irish extraction who tilled an unforgiving plot near Painted Post, a one-horse town in the wilds of New York State.[2] He did better in the lumber business – well enough to give TJ a decent education – though his ungrateful son refused to work the family farm. Tom wanted to go into business, but after making a pig's ear of an upmarket butcher's shop he soon thought better of it. He tried teaching; he lasted one day. He turned to selling and toured the countryside hawking pianos, organs, and sewing machines, all unsuccessfully. He moved to Buffalo, but couldn't sell himself sufficiently convincingly to get a job. When he finally struck lucky with another firm of sewing-machine manufacturers, he was sacked before he'd even got his feet on the treadle. He then hooked up with a blowhard conman called C. B. Barron, who persuaded TJ to invest in diverse dubious schemes courtesy of money borrowed from his father, and promptly disappeared with the loot.

Tom, Tom, the foolish farmer's son finally turned up at the Buffalo branch of National Cash Register, a.k.a. "The Cash," though his track record was so poor that the manager spurned his application. Repeatedly. After numerous attempts at persuasion, Watson talked John Range into giving him a two-week trial. Happy day! Only he didn't sell a single cash register. Beaten but unbowed, TJ reported back that he had "some good business in sight." Far from being impressed, Range launched into a tirade that changed Watson's life: "In sight? How far away is it? Can I see it? Don't you ever waste my time by talking about business that's 'in sight.' I am not interested until you can show it to me in the form of a signed order."

Instead of showing the shy, stammering, and somewhat tongue-tied youngster the door, Range took him under his wing. He taught Tom the rudiments of NCR's renowned selling system – a features and benefits classic – and the Red Sea of sales suddenly parted. Armed with a surefire script that overcame his conversational difficulties in unstructured selling situations, The Cash's latest recruit sold like billy-o. Within a month, he was as good as his mentor. Within a couple of years, he was the best in the company, which was the best of the best at the time. So ruthless was Watson in pursuit of a sale – physical intimidation of prospects came with the territory – that he was put in charge of The Cash's dirty-tricks department, which ran competitors out of business by whatever means necessary.

He was indicted in 1912, along with the entire upper echelon of NCR, and sentenced to a year in prison for "flagrant commercial piracy." Naturally, he appealed and eventually won his case, but in the meantime he'd been cashiered by The Cash.

Within six months of his sacking, Watson was appointed general manager of the Computing-Tabulating-Recording Company, a debt-laden mishmash of unrelated product lines: everything from butchers' scales and cheese-cutting machines to automatic punch clocks for hourly paid employees. Recognizing that the future lay in "tabulation" – the management of business information – Watson quickly turned CTR into a lean mean selling machine. He did so by emulating and eventually surpassing the sales system he'd been taught at NCR: ambitious quotas, guaranteed sales territories, strict codes of personal conduct, carefully honed scripts for every conceivable selling situation, extravagant expense accounts to convey the impression of unalloyed success, and not least a brutally competitive, sell-sell-sell corporate culture that not only convinced the reps they were the best of the best but galvanized them into proving it. By the time CTR changed its name to IBM in 1924, TJ was firmly established as a man of men, the world's greatest salesman, and the father of a ten-year-old boy, Thomas J. Watson Jr, who spent his entire life obsessed with the fear of failure. But that's another story ...

Double Triple A

So what can we learn from the Thomas Watsons of this world? Overcoming failure aside, is there anything that connects the people in this book? What do they share across the yawning gulfs of culture, gender, sector, and historical epoch? More to the point, is it possible to summarize their shared characteristics in a memorable way, if only because books like this one demand a glib, ideally alliterative, happy-clappy climactic checklist?

Hmmm. Hesitant as I am to come up with a one-size-fits-all inventory, since every Fail Better hero is unique, it is possible to pick out several shared characteristics, all conveniently beginning with "A."

Ambition. Thomas Watson, if not quite a megalomaniacal despot, set out to make Big Blue the biggest and the best. In 1926, he rallied his troops with the stirring words "This business of ours has a future ... Nothing in the world will ever stop it. The IBM is not merely an organization of men; it is an institution that will go on forever."[3] He meant what he said, moreover. He aimed to build an unbeatable business. This is true of all our FIBs. Donald Trump's vaunting ambition is emblazed on every building he's ever constructed. P. T. Barnum had his Greatest Show on Earth. Edward Bernays' PR approach was predicated on hugely ambitious ideas – what his biographer calls "Big Think." Akio Morita wanted everyone in the world to own a Sony Walkman, and to this day his company considers itself "Like no other." The monumental scale of Jeff Koons' art, such as *Puppy* outside Bilbao Guggenheim, testifies to the rampant egomania that lurks behind his diffident exterior. When Madonna was interviewed on *American Bandstand* at the start of her career, Dick Clark asked the wannabe pop star what her ambitions were. "To rule the world," Madonna replied. She meant it, too.

Activity. It's impossible to overstate the sheer physical effort that FIBs put into their endeavours. Trite as it is to say there's no substitute for hard work, it's true all the same. Thomas Watson was an elbow-grease monkey who worked stupendously long hours, didn't retire till a month before his death at the age of 82, and famously attributed his success to the fact that he tried more often, failed more often, and eventually struck lucky.[4] Ron Popeil's status as the salesman of the century was based, he firmly believed, on those early, early starts and long,

long days at Maxwell Street market. The sheer energy, the effort, the never-say-die enthusiasm he put into every sales pitch was palpable. Rupert Murdoch may be 76 years old but he remains a hands-on, ass-kicking, hard-grinding ball-buster whose eerie 3 a.m. calls put the fear of God into his News Corp. minions. Anton Mesmer pulled out all the stops on his glass harmonica to promote animal magnetism, a revolutionary therapeutic system that's still in use today. After a fashion. Vijay Mallya strikes many as a fun-loving party animal, a bit of a big-haired dilettante, yet he works extremely hard creating the playboy image that sells his aspirational lifestyle brand. Well, that's his excuse and he's sticking to it.

Astigmatism. All marketers are familiar with the notion of marketing myopia: companies' inability to see what business they're really in (transportation rather than railroads, entertainment not movies, ¾ inch holes instead of ¾ inch drills, etc.) As a rule, myopia isn't the issue with FIBs, though success-bred arrogance can tempt them to take their eye off the marketplace prize. What they share, rather, is astigmatism: the quirky ability to see what competitors can't, plus the willingness to act on their instinct. Sam Walton saw the opportunities for small-town discount stores and built an unbeatable business while his rivals looked the other way. Coco Chanel sensed the latent demand for less formal, constricting, and elaborate outfits, and by replacing bustles, stays, and suchlike with a simple relaxed look, she changed the face of fashion for ever. In a world where basic foodstuffs were sold in a high-price, high-margin, low-turnover manner, Thomas Lipton knew in his waters that low price, low margin, high turnover was the way to go. When Thomas Watson took over CTR in 1914, he was faced with a hodgepodge of unrelated products, yet he could see that the most unprofitable part of the business, tabulating machines, had the greatest long-term potential. He bet the farm on information management and reaped the cornucopian marketing rewards.

Amplification. There are many ambitious individuals. Hard workers are ten a penny. The world is full of individuals with fantastic off-kilter ideas. Much less common is the ability to stand out from the crowd. That's where our FIBs are unsurpassed. They get people talking. They are larger than life. They are prodigious self-promoters one and all. They stir up controversy. They know that free publicity is priceless. They keep themselves in the public eye. Michael O'Leary is never reluctant to make a fool of himself provided Ryanair gets a plug for its latest route, price promotion, or crush-the-competition manoeuvre. Lola Montez's willingness to horsewhip all and sundry – Prussian cavalrymen, theatre managers, imbecilic aristocrats – was legendary, as were her scandalous sexual exploits and shameless box-office-busting behaviour. André Citroën lit up the Eiffel Tower for a decade, hired sky-writing aircraft to spell out his name in vapour trails, and gambled his way to glorious oblivion. Aimee Semple McPherson had her own radio station in the days when radio ruled the waves, once astonished the assembled multitudes by riding a motorbike down the aisle of her Angelus Temple, and then pulled off that unforgettable disappearing act. Thomas Watson was a publicity hound who happily put himself about on behalf of Big Blue. His stage-managed rallies for IBM's foot soldiers were a sight to behold: white-collar evangelism in excelsis. He also had a thing about cross-dressing, but we won't go into that.

Aphorism. Another remarkable characteristic that FIBs unfailingly share, along with an aversion to self-effacement and the searing insight that sets them apart from the common marketing herd, is encapsulation. They are blessed with an aphoristic bent, the ability to sum up everything they stand for in a memorable saying or pithy turn of phrase. As every astute marketer appreciates, it's hard to beat a good slogan. It appeals to the public, it energizes the troops, it is ineradicably inscribed in the collective memory banks. "The pause that refreshes." "Where's the beef?" "Finger-lickin' good." "Stick to the knitting." "Show me the money." "Jesus saves." Thomas Watson was uncommonly partial to soundbites and they echoed and re-echoed around IBM. "Think" was his all-time favourite. It followed him from NCR to CTR to Big Blue, an aphorism in itself. It was incised on every available surface, and woe betide the facility that didn't display "Think" prominently when TJ dropped in for a friendly visit. Gabriele d'Annunzio was no slouch with the epithets either, though what *me no prego* lacked in propriety, it gained in pith and punch. Trevor Beattie's entire career is encapsulated in the advertising straplines "Hello boys" and "FCUK." Steve Jobs urges his silicon stormtroopers to "Think different" and "Make a dent in the universe." Dale Carnegie sold millions of books that consist essentially of a congeries of aphorisms in a cogently titled package. Duveen sold multi-million-dollar paintings on the basis of a single word: Duveen. A sidelong glance from Anna Held said it all. And then some.

Ambiguity. The beauty of "Think" or indeed any of the other memorable marketing memes is that they contain a bit of semantic wriggle-room. That is to say, their meaning is inherently ambiguous. What does "Think" mean, exactly? What does the "it" in "Coke is it" refer to? Isn't "Fail better" an oxymoron? Samuel Beckett refused to answer such questions, leaving the reader/theatre-goer to decide. Thomas Watson never elaborated on "Think" because he believed spelling out its meaning destroyed its mystique. Robert Goizueta, the Coke kingpin during its early-eighties heyday, was quite specific about the importance of ambiguity.[5] "It" created a space for consumer fantasizing in much the same way that manikins in display windows used to be faceless so that consumers could project themselves into the outfits (the silhouettes in iPod ads perform a similar function). Success in marketing often involves an element of uncertainty, inscrutability, incongruity, equivocation. There's no doubt that much of McKinsey's appeal is attributable to the cult-like mystique that Marvin Bower built around his enigmatic organization. Mason Locke Weems sold an incongruous mix of piety and profanity. Madonna is famous for her restless mutability, infuriating capriciousness, and ever-changing ambiguity. Thomas Watson was an absolute monster, a tyrant of Louis B. Meyer proportions. At the same time, he was capable of benevolence beyond the call of duty and remarkable acts of uncalled-for generosity that earned the undying loyalty of his workforce. He was an enigma bubble-wrapped in a mystery, vacuum-packed in a riddle, and hermetically sealed in a styrofoam-padded paradox.

Dialectical Marketing

The enigmatic, inherently contradictory character of IBM under Watson is evident in many outstanding marketing organizations: Microsoft under Gates, Virgin under Branson, Oracle under Ellison, Revlon under Revson, GM under Durant, Xerox under Wilson, Coke under Woodruff, Amazon under Bezos, Body Shop under Roddick. Such contradictions, it must be stressed, are the cause of their success rather than obstacles to be overcome or excised. Management is a dialectical process, a hopscotch-like ability to leap from grand vision to fine detail, from past glories to future prospects, from local focus to global domination, from customer needs to corporate capabilities, from following the pack to leading the charge, from tooth-and-nail competition to cooperating in everyone's best interests.

However, of all the dialectical tensions that FIB managers must negotiate, three are particularly noteworthy:

Sales versus marketing. It can't have escaped your notice that many of our FIBs are described as great salespersons, and everyone knows that there's more to marketing than sales. Indeed, the tension between the two is legendary. While it is true that marketing and sales aren't synonymous, it's also true that marketing ultimately boils down to selling stuff. Advertising, distribution, package design, brand personality, market research, etc. etc. etc. are all fine and dandy – and vitally necessary, furthermore – but unless someone *buys* the product or service or idea or whatever, all our marketing efforts are in vain. Boiling marketing down to "selling stuff" may seem crude and reductive, but in a world where every organization is marketing oriented and every organization unctuously promises to love, honour, and obey the customer till death do them part, many of today's marketing-savvy consumers prefer to deal with organizations that openly admit their profit-making motivation rather than hypocritically claim that they really, really care about customers' welfare. As Ryanair under O'Leary epitomizes, twenty-first-century marketers should do exactly what it says on the tin.

Structure versus agency. Even though marketing is something that is done by and for people, the people who actually do it are strangely absent from most mainstream marketing books. The emphasis is very much on "structure" rather than "agency," whether it be the elements of the external environment or the components of the marketing mix or the five forces that affect a company's competitive context or the various stages of the innovation diffusion/product development/advertising awareness process. Although the "great man" school of thought has fallen into disrepute among feminists, historians, postmodernists, organization theorists, leadership analysts, and the like, there is no question that active, ambitious, astigmatic, amplification-minded individuals make a *very real* difference in the Fail Better derby. Marketing mounts need a jockey, and no amount of academic handicapping will change that. Apple went to pot without Jobs.[6] Oracle without Ellison is hard to imagine.

Ben & Jerry's lost its cool when Ben and Jerry sold out. Sam Walton's ghost is alive and well and hustling in Bentonville. Will Dell go to hell without its main man? Will Virgin abandon its virtue after Branson? What will happen to News Corp. when Rupert Murdoch finally bows out? Does Calvin Klein have anything under its kingpin? Now, none of this means that human agency is the only thing that matters. But to imagine that great men and great women don't make a massive difference is to misunderstand the nature of management. So important is agency that if a charismatic frontperson doesn't exist, the organization has to invent one: Bibendum, Ronald McDonald, Ms Chiquita Banana, the Marlboro Man.

Presence versus absence. Presence is all, or so traditional textbooks suggest. The key to successful marketing is to make our product or service available at the right time in the right place at the right price in the right size with the right point-of-sale support, after-sales service, advertising campaign, and so on. Coca-Cola's determination to be within "arm's reach of desire" encapsulates this marketing mindset. Important as presence is, however, absence is crucial too. Absence makes the heart grow fonder, and in many circumstances the best way of turning a customer into a lustomer – someone who absolutely adores what you're selling – is to deny their demands, disdain their advances, dilate their desires. Absence, remember, is a much more powerful motivator than presence. When something is perpetually present and easily attainable, it loses its allure and becomes a ho-hum commodity. Familiarity breeds contempt. But when that very same something is suddenly withdrawn or lacking or almost unattainable or available only for a limited time, all hell breaks loose. The single biggest boost Coca-Cola ever received was when the carbonated nectar was difficult to obtain during the Second World War.[7] Duveen's *Blue Boy* escapade also epitomizes this propensity, as does Barnum's Jumbo jamboree, as do the here-today-gone-tomorrow apparel offers of Zara, Primark, or H&M. Now, this is not just a case of "treat 'em mean to keep 'em keen," though that is undeniably part of denial marketing's power. There must be something to make them keen in the first place; without presence, absence can't work its motivational magic. Yes, we have to be there for customers, but we have to be unattainable too.[8]

Three to Go

What I'm saying, in conclusion, is that there's more to fail-better marketing than *Ambition, Activity, Astigmatism, Amplification, Aphorism,* and *Ambiguity.* Accident (sheer luck is a factor), Abandonment (many of our FIBs were orphans), and Appearance (let's be honest, allure has a lot to do with it) could easily be added to our A-list. No matter how long the list, however, attributes are insufficient in themselves. We can't understand marketing, much less the Fail Better process, by identifying its component parts. True, traditional marketing textbooks and how-to management tomes are inordinately fond of checklists and inventories – 3Cs, 4Ps, 7Ss, SWOT, PEST, AIDA, etc. – but you'll never fail better by ticking the appropriate boxes. It is only by hopscotching across the marketing minefield that calamitous failure can be deferred.

Not avoided.

Only deferred.

Because everything fails in the end.

I'm conscious, of course, that "do the dialectical spider-dance" isn't much of a take-away. Readers of marketing books, even unorthodox ones like this, rightly expect more for their money than postmodern platitudes. (Postmodern platitudes are my speciality, admittedly, and I make no apology for them. At a time when "modern" marketing platitudes still hold sway – the customer is king, there's riches in niches – a moment of postmodern provocation isn't unwelcome.) In fairness, though,

I didn't promise you an all-singing alternative to the conventional marketing concept, only an inkling of an alternative. And I believe that our dialectical A-list represents the tinkling of an inkling.

Let me conclude, therefore, with three final thumbnail sketches of fail-better heroes, individuals who succeeded by refusing to follow the rules, fall into line, or run with the pack:

★ Thomas Watson Jr had big shoes to fill: those of the "world's greatest salesman," Thomas Watson Sr. He tried them on for size when he joined the family firm, but they neither fitted properly nor suited his playboy lifestyle. Indeed, he was so utterly useless at everything he did – we're talkin' classic rich-kid wastrel – that he not only earned the nickname Terrible Tom but thoroughly deserved it. During his interwar stint at Big Blue, the boss's son couldn't cope with even the most elementary corporate tasks. He failed worse rather than better and would have continued to do so had the Second World War not intervened. A keen amateur pilot, he volunteered for the US Air Force, served with considerable distinction, and returned to IBM in 1946 his own man. Tom quickly demonstrated that he was a silicon chip off the old block. He took the reins on his father's retirement in 1956 and, thanks to the computer revolution of the 1960s, eventually eclipsed TJ's incredible marketing accomplishments. The development of the groundbreaking IBM 360 series in particular was one of the greatest Hail Mary plays in the history of American business. Although IBM went to pieces after Terrible Tom's departure (as per the summary in chapter 1), Thomas Watson Jr richly deserved *Fortune*'s obituary accolade: "the greatest capitalist of all time."

★ Samuel Beckett, similarly, was an abject failure for most of his adult life. Having spurned the family construction business, rejected a potentially lucrative career in advertising, and abandoned a comfortable teaching post at Trinity College, Dublin, he became a penniless poet in interwar Paris, that famously bohemian destination where the Lost Generation went to find itself. He joined the James Joyce set and penned occasional poems, novels, translations, and works of literary criticism, all of which evaporated unnoticed into the no-account ether. If it hadn't been for handouts from his father and the succour of his younger brother, who took over the family firm after his father's sudden death, Sam couldn't have afforded to fail for so long. He was almost 50 years old when he took a break from novel writing, dashed off a tragicomic play about the unending agonies of existence, managed to get it staged thanks to a French government grant and very low production costs, and then awoke to find that *Waiting for Godot* had made him a world-famous literary superstar and, later, a fail-better spokesperson.

★ Sir Winston Churchill, recently voted the greatest Briton of the twentieth century, was a serial failure – a congenital failure, in fact. He failed to shine at school, he failed to get into Sandhurst on three occasions, he repeatedly failed to get elected to parliament, and he failed abysmally as Home Secretary, President of the Board of Trade, and First Lord of the Admiralty, where he was responsible for the disastrous Dardanelles campaign. Come the mid-1930s, he was widely considered a hopeless case, with a lamentable track record and a capacity for alcoholic beverages that makes George Best look like a teetotaller. But then along came Hitler, whereupon Churchill's finest hour began. Granted, it didn't last too long; Winston's post-war political performance was less than illustrious. However, he succeeded when it really, really, really mattered. "Success," he once observed, "is the ability to go from one failure to another with no loss of enthusiasm." True enough, but what is the ultimate secret of the greatest Briton's success? Winston had something to say about that, too: "Never give in, never give in, never, never, never, never – in nothing, great or small, large or petty – never give in except to convictions of honour and good sense. Never, never, never, never give up."

Or as W. C. Fields puts it, "If at first you don't succeed, try, try again. Then quit. No use being a damn fool about it."

★ NOTES AND REFERENCES ★

An Introductory Kick in the Teeth

1. Felix Dennis, *How to Get Rich* (Ebury Press, London, 2006, p. 38). Due to space limitations, I've kept my notes and references to a minimum. Many of the quotes are unattributed, though I'm happy to provide citations on request. Feel free to get in touch. I can be contacted via my website: www.sfxbrown.com.

2. Clarence, incidentally, was also an amateur opera singer of some renown. Naturally, his signature aria was "My tiny brand is frozen." Only kidding.

1   The Failgood Factor

1. See my "Fail Better! Samuel Beckett's secrets of business and branding success," *Business Horizons*, 49 (2), 2006, pp. 161–9. The classic quote is from Beckett's *Worstward Ho*.

2. Donald W. Hendon, *Classic Failures in Product Marketing: Marketing Principles Violations and How to Avoid Them* (NTC Business Books, Lincolnwood, Ill., 1992, p. 5).

3. I sourced most of these from a fantastic little self-help book by Herter Studio. It's called *Fail Better*, believe it or not. I came across the book after starting work on my own *Fail Better!* Honest, I did. I swear to you. Cross my heart and …

4. There are many fine books on business failures. Examples include: Paul Ormerod, *Why Most Things Fail: Evolution, Extinction and Economics* (Faber and Faber, London, 2005); Sydney Finkelstein, *Why Smart Executives Fail: And What You Can Learn From Their Mistakes* (Portfolio, New York, 2003);

Geoff Tibballs, *Business Blunders: Dirty Dealing and Financial Failure in the World of Big Business* (Robinson Publishing, London, 1999); Carl Franklin, *Why Innovation Fails: Hard-Won Lessons For Business* (Spiro Press, London, 2003); and, especially good from an historical perspective, Scott A. Sandage, *Born Losers: A History of Failure in America* (Harvard University Press, Cambridge, Mass., 2005). The classic marketing text is Robert F. Harley's *Marketing Mistakes*, which has gone through numerous editions (e.g. Wiley, New York, 2001). Also valuable is Matt Haig's *Brand Failures: The Truth About the 100 Biggest Branding Mistakes of All Time* (Kogan Page, London, 2003). Other related contributions – enough already, guys! – include Michael E. Raynor, *The Strategy Paradox* (Currency, New York, 2007), Jeffrey Sonnenfeld and Andrew Ward, *Firing Back: How Great Leaders Rebound After Career Disasters* (Harvard Business School Press, Boston, 2007), and Jadish N. Sheth, *The Self-Destructive Habits of Good Companies ... And How to Break Them* (Warton School Publishing, Upper Saddle River, 2007).

5.   The Tupperware story is well worth studying in detail. Check out Alison J. Clarke, *Tupperware: The Promise of Plastic in 1950s America* (Smithsonian Institution Press, Washington, 1999).

6.   These examples are sourced from Hendon (*op. cit.*) and *The Economist, A Business Miscellany* (Profile Books, London, 2006, especially pp. 19–26).

7.   Richard Farson and Ralph Keyes, *The Innovation Paradox: The Success of Failure, The Failure of Success* (Free Press, New York, 2002).

8.   Danny Miller, *The Icarus Paradox: How Exceptional Companies Bring About Their Own Downfall* (HarperBusiness, New York, 1990).

9.   Boo.com, wouldn't you know it, has recently made something of a comeback. Apparently, it's being relaunched as a travel-cum-social networking website. Watch this (cyber) space.

2 Bring on the Empty Marketers

1. David Niven, *Bring on the Empty Horses* (Coronet Books, London, 1977). See also his earlier autobiographical classic, *The Moon's a Balloon* (Putnam, New York, 1972).

2. I've worried this one to death in various published articles. I won't belabour it with a citation, much less chapter and verse. Fairly typical is my contribution to the anthology *Does Marketing Need Reform?* (see note 10 below).

3. This list is adapted, yet again, from Hendon (*op. cit.*, p. 3). Also noteworthy is the recent cover story by Jena McGregor in *BusinessWeek* ("How failure breeds success," 10 July 2006, pp. 42–52). Well worth reading, this discusses several calamitous soft drinks including Choglit, OK Soda and Surge. Enjoy.

4. The Booz Allen & Hamilton study is cogently summarised in Franklin (*op. cit.*, pp. 39–40).

5. In a wonderfully ironic quirk, one of the dragons on *Dragons' Den*, Peter Jones, developed a spin-off show called *Tycoon*. Its USP was that the "innovative" products from the show were to be made available from stand-alone retail stores, also called Tycoon. Do I really have to go on? I think you know where this one's heading ...

6. Haldane's classic comment is quoted in Ormerod (*op. cit.*, p. 156).

7. These examples are considered in detail in Haig (*op. cit.*).

8. You've heard of lad-lit and chick-lit, as well as their raunchier cousins dick-lit and clit-lit? Well, there's a whole new genre out there called fail-lit. Its best-known exponent is Lynne Truss, whose book on our inability to punctuate properly, *Eats, Shoots & Leaves*, sold some three million copies worldwide. She followed *Eats* up with a screed on rudeness – our failure to treat people with common courtesy. Truss has stimulated countless copycat books, all of which focus on failure's manifold manifestations: spelling, sex, slang, service in shops and, courtesy of Richard Dawkins, the shortcomings of organized religion (*The God Delusion*). Jared Diamond goes one better with *Collapse*, a detailed comparative analysis of why entire societies decline. We're doomed, I tell you. Doomed!

9.   Another cracker in the same vein is Coors' celebrated advertising slogan "Turn it loose," which when translated (again) into Spanish (again) announced (unforgettably) "Suffers from diarrhoea." I could go on ... let me see ... there's the Sinclair C5 ... the Segway Personal Transporter ... the Sony Aibo Robot ... the Microsoft Zune ... the Amstrad Emailer ... enough!

10.   Jagdish N. Sheth and Rajendra S. Sisodia (eds.), *Does Marketing Need Reform? Fresh Perspectives on the Future* (M. E. Sharpe, Armonk, NY, 2006).

3 The Best of the Worst

1.   In case you think I'm being catty – I am not in the least bit envious of his books' huge sales – I should point out that Jim Collins' supposedly rigorous research methodology is anything but. The methods employed in *Good to Great* and *Built to Last* are highly subjective. There's nothing wrong with subjectivity, but Collins masquerades as an objective, dispassionate researcher, presumably because "rigor" sells better. Mmmeeeooowww!

2.   See my "Ryanair: The Cu Chulainn of Civil Aviation," *Journal of Strategic Marketing*, 14 (1), 2006, pp. 45–55. FYI, this article was written under the pseudonym Brian Boru. Not that I'm afraid of O'Leary or anything. Afraid of flying Ryanair, possibly, but the man himself? I don't think so. There are two excellent books on Ryanair and its main man: Siobhan Creaton, *Ryanair: How a Small Irish Airline Conquered Europe* (Aurum, London, 2004) and Alan Ruddock, *Michael O'Leary: A Life in Full Flight* (Penguin Ireland, Dublin, 2007).

3.   This quote is from Graham Bowley, "How Low Can You Go?" *Financial Times Magazine*, 21 June 2003, pp. 16–23.

4.   Wal-Mart has stimulated a mini-literary genre all to itself. Wal-lit, perhaps? My principal sources were Sam's ghostwritten

autobiography *Made in America* (Bantam, New York, 1993) and Bob Ortega, *In Sam We Trust: The Untold Story of Sam Walton and How Wal-Mart is Devouring the World* (Kogan Page, London, 1999). The "not cut out for retail" remark is on p. 23 of *Made in America*.

5.   David Rowan, "The Next Big Thing: Flogs," *The Times Magazine*, 11 November 2006, p. 12.

6.   See Larry Tye, *The Father of Spin: Edward L. Bernays and the Birth of Public Relations* (Crown, New York, 1998).

7.   Edward L. Bernays, *biography of an idea: memoirs of public relations counsel Edward L. Bernays* (Simon & Schuster, New York, 1965). The title on the original volume, incidentally, is in lower case. Eddie wanted a talking-point, I guess. Or maybe he was on an e.e. cummings trip at the time.

8.   The incomparable Duveen has been treated to an in-depth biographical treatment by Meryle Secrest (*Duveen: A Life in Art*, University of Chicago Press, Chicago, Ill., 2004). Much more fun is S. N. Behrman's 1950s pen-portrait (*Duveen*, The Little Bookroom, New York, 1951), which began life as a series of articles in *The New Yorker*.

9.   S. N. Behrman (*op. cit.*, p. 66).

10.   My source for Ms Montez's incredible escapades was Bruce Seymour, *Lola Montez: A Life* (Yale University Press, New Haven, Conn., 1995). Seymour was so enamoured by the minx that he used his winnings on the game show *Jeopardy!* to support his quixotic quest. During the writing of *Fail Better!*, another full-length life story of Lola appeared (James Morton, *Lola Montez: Her Life and Conquests*, Portrait, London, 2007). I haven't had a chance to read it yet.

11.   Elizabeth Haas Edersheim, *McKinsey's Marvin Bower: Vision, Leadership, and the Creation of Management Consulting* (Wiley, New York, 2004). All of the quotes in this section are from Edersheim's biography. The only exception is the last one ("We do not learn from clients"), which is from Stuart Crainer, *The*

Ultimate Business Guru Book: 50 Thinkers Who Made Management (Capstone, Oxford, 1998, p. 24).

12. As for Virgin Atlantic's recent decision to blow the whistle on its fuel-surcharge cartel with British Airways, what can I say? I don't know which is more obnoxious, the price-fixing itself or spilling the beans on BA to avoid prosecution. "No one," as *The Independent on Sunday* put it, "likes a sneak."

13. The classic hatchet job on "Rupert the Fear" is Bruce Page, *The Murdoch Archipelago* (Simon & Schuster, London, 2003). Actually, Page goes so far over the top it's hard not to sympathize with the Dirty Digger. The marketing angle on Murdoch is well covered by Stuart Crainer, *Business the Rupert Murdoch Way* (Capstone, Oxford, 2002).

14. John Nathan, *Sony: The Private Life* (HarperCollins, London, 2000). See also Shu Shin Luh, *Business the Sony Way: Secrets of the World's Most Innovative Electronics Giant* (Capstone, Oxford, 2003). Sony's movie escapades are cogently described in Nancy Griffin and Kim Masters, *Hit and Run – How Jon Peters and Peter Gruber Took Sony for a Ride in Hollywood* (Simon and Schuster, London, 1996).

15. Nathan (*op. cit.*, p. 78).

16. Punishing failure was considered counterproductive in Morita's Sony; he believed it reduced people's willingness to take risks and engendered a conservative corporate culture. Morita's successor, Norio Ohga, maintained the fail-better tradition, most notably with PlayStation, which encountered enormous internal opposition, suffered Trinitron-scale developmental difficulties and faced deeply entrenched competitors, Nintendo and Sega. Yet in keeping with the Morita mindset, Ohga backed Ken Kutaragi, the maverick video-games lover who wouldn't say die and whose quantum-leap product subsequently scooped the pixilated pool.

17. Daniel Mark Epstein, *Sister Aimee: The Life of Aimee Semple McPherson* (Harcourt Brace, San Diego, 1993).

18. Even H. L. Mencken, the celebrated scourge of the "booboisie" who hated organized religion so much he routinely stole Gideon Bibles from hotel rooms and sent them to friends signed "With the Compliments of the Author," was uncharacteristically undecided about Ms McPherson. In his influential newspaper column, Mencken drew attention to "her shiny eyes, her mahogany hair, her eloquent hips and her lascivious voice." Not that undecided, clearly.

19. John Reynolds, *André Citroën: The Man and the Motor Cars* (Sutton Publishing, Stroud, 1996).

20. James Mackay, *The Man Who Invented Himself: A Life of Sir Thomas Lipton* (Mainstream Publishing, Edinburgh, 1998). As the title suggests, this biography unpicks all the stories surrounding Sir Thomas, mostly those he concocted himself.

21. Mackay (*ibid.*) reckons Tommy was the only gay in the Gorbals.

22. John Woodhouse, *Gabriele d'Annunzio: Defiant Archangel* (Oxford University Press, Oxford, 2001). See also Anthony Rhodes, *The Poet as Superman: A Life of Gabriele d'Annunzio* (Weidenfeld and Nicolson, London, 1959).

23. *Primo vere* also benefited from a characteristically OTT publicity stunt – the first of many – in which d'Annunzio faked his own death. In a horse-riding accident. Gabriele issued a distressing press release under the pseudonym G. Rutani and gleefully read the extensive media coverage of a promising poet's untimely end. The obituaries unfailingly mentioned that *Primo vere* was available from all good bookstores. It sold well and was widely reviewed, though the reaction of d'Annunzio's parents to their sixteen-year-old son's alleged demise went unrecorded.

24. Eve Golden, *Anna Held and the Birth of Ziegfeld's Broadway* (University Press of Kentucky, Lexington, 2000).

25. Giles Kemp and Edward Claflin, *Dale Carnegie: The Man Who Influenced Millions* (St Martin's Press, New York, 1989). The book itself is also worth reading, though I'm not exactly an advertisement for its interpersonal promises: Dale Carnegie, *How to Win Friends and Influence People* (Pocket Books, New York, 1981).

26. For further details of the Vicary scam, see my *Marketing: The Retro Revolution* (Sage, London, 2001). Yes, I'm conscious of the irony implicit in my "sleepy, sleepy" subtitle. My prose has that effect on people.

27. There are many books on mesmerism. My main source was Derek Forrest, *The Evolution of Hypnotism* (Black Ace Books, Forfar, 1999). Another outstanding text is Alison Winter, *Mesmerized: Powers of Mind in Victorian Britain* (University of Chicago Press, Chicago, 1998).

28. Anton wrote several learned papers on the subject, only to have them plagiarized by the unforgettably named cleric Father Hell.

29. Most of the books on Jeff Koons are exhibition catalogues; there's no proper biography. So the sources for this pen portrait are many and varied, too many and varied to list. I suggest you go see his work instead. Photographs don't do it justice. Actually, it's kind of creepy in the flesh.

30. This artwork, incidentally, was filled with whiskey by the Jim Beam people and has the bonded-warehouse sticker to prove it. Mind you, it's a shame that Yuan and Xi, the artworld pranksters who pissed in Duchamp's *Fountain*, didn't elect to crack open the Koons and quaff its contents. At the very least, the alcoholic diuretic would've fuelled their Duchamp pisstake.

31. Okay, okay, I invented the bit about fcuk condoms. Mind you, you never know. Condoms seem like such an obvious fcuk brand extension that they must have been available at some stage. Check it out for yourself, if you wish. I'd prefer not to go there, thanks all the same.

32. There are numerous newspaper and magazine articles about Beattie. He employs his own PR person, which is unusual for an adman. Fairly typical is Harriet Lane, "Beattie mania," *The Observer Magazine*, 28 January 2001, pp. 10–14. Clever Trevor's latest wheeze, which emerged after this book was completed, is "starvertising." This involves acquiring the naming rights to 628 stars (night sky stars, that is) which together form the shape of

the logo of Npower, a UK electricity and gas supplier. To boldly logo, eh?

33. Axel Madsen, *Chanel: A Woman of Her Own* (Henry Holt, New York, 1990).

34. This Nazi allusion is not accidental. Coco was accused of collaboration during the Second World War, when she had a torrid affair with a German intelligence officer. She also got involved in espionage, believe it or not. Toward the end of the fighting, she acted as a Nazi intermediary in Operation *Modellhut*, which was a top-secret attempt by senior army officers to negotiate a peace treaty with Churchill. Chanel's mission to Madrid was a shambles, however. She was later arrested during the *épuration* – the barbaric post-liberation purge of presumed collaborators – but was released without charge, allegedly on Churchill's say-so. Coco knew too much about the English upper crust for comfort, and a trial might have opened a can of Windsor worms.

35. Ron Popeil, *The Salesman of the Century* (Delacorte Press, New York, 1995). The classic pitchman's countdown is explicated in the excellent (and beautifully illustrated) book on Ronco by Timothy Samuelson, *But Wait! There's More! The Irresistible Appeal and Spiel of Ronco and Popeil* (Rizzoli International, New York, 2002).

36. Lewis Leary, *The Book-Peddling Parson: An Account of the Life and Works of Mason Locke Weems, Patriot, Pitchman, Author and Purveyor of Morality to the Citizenry of the Early United States of America* (Algonquin Books, Chapel Hill, NC, 1984).

37. Weems' sinsploitation was bad enough, but he illustrated his publications with spectacularly gruesome engravings that gave readers a transgressive thrill coupled with a hint of holier-than-thou prurience. One of his letters to Carey inquires about the possibility of finding "some artist good at design who would give us at once the likeness of a very beautiful woman distorted or convulsed with Diabolical possession, in the act of murdering, with uplifted axe, her sleeping husband". Where's Lola Montez when you need her?

38. Still available from all good remainder bins, charity shops and second-hand bookstores.

39. Donald Trump, *The Art of the Deal* (Random House, New York, 1987). There are many biographies of The Donald, good, bad and indifferent. A recent addition is the hagiographic volume by Robert Slater, *No Such Thing as Over-Exposure* (Pearson–Prentice Hall, Upper Saddle River, NJ, 2005).

40. As with Trump, there are dozens of books on Madonna. I'll spare you the details, though you may want to track down the cartoon version of her life story: Peter Robinson, *A Girl Called Madonna* (Friday Books, London, 2006).

41. FYI, Maverick Records was founded by Madonna and her then manager Freddy DeMann in 1991. Its signings included Alanis Morissette, the Prodigy and Muse. A legal battle broke out with Warner Brothers in 2004 that resulted in their acquiring Maverick as a wholly-owned subsidiary.

42. My main source for this section is the inflammatory biography of Jobs by Jeffrey S. Young and William L. Simon, *iCon: Steve Jobs, the Greatest Second Act in the History of Business* (Wiley, New York, 2005).

43. See James B. Twitchell, *Twenty Ads That Shook the World* (Three Rivers Press, New York, 2000).

44. Jeffrey S. Young and William L. Simon (*op. cit.*, p. 224).

45. Yes, I know it's a saffron not an orange stripe on the Indian flag, but allow me some poetic licence, for goodness' sake!

46. There's no biography of Mallya as yet, though his life story is so colourful that it can't be long a-comin'. This pen portrait was pulled together from various websites and press articles.

47. Joe Vitale, *There's a Customer Born Every Minute: P.T. Barnum's Secrets to Business Success* (Amacom, New York, 1998).

48. The autobiography's still in print and well worth reading. Barnum, BTW, was a contemporary of Lola Montez. At one stage, he considered managing her – she was the biggest attraction around by far – but thought better of it in the end. More's the pity.

49. The woolly horse and buffalo hunt stunts are described in most Barnum biographies. By far the best illustrated of these is Philip B. Kundhardt, Jr, Philip B. Kundhardt III, and Peter W. Kundhardt, *P.T. Barnum: America's Greatest Showman* (Knopf, New York, 1995).

4   Who's the Daddy?

1. See Janet Lunn, *Maud's House of Dreams: The Life of Lucy Maud Montgomery* (Doubleday, Toronto, 2002).

2. Stephen Brown, *Marketing: The Retro Revolution* (*op. cit.*).

3. Santa has recently been treated to a biography: Jeremy Seal, *Santa: A Life* (Picador, London, 2006). It's not very good, though. Much better is Russell W. Belk's "Materialism and the Modern U.S. Christmas" in Elizabeth C. Hirschman, *Interpretive Consumer Research* (Association for Consumer Research, Provo, UT, 1989, pp. 136–47).

5   Playing Hopscotch in the Marketing Minefield

1. Watson, incidentally, wasn't the first to be so described. Nor the last. "Diamond" Jim Brady, the opalescent king of the railroad age, received the "greatest salesman" accolade a generation earlier. It's since been bestowed on Joe Girard, the phenomenal Motown "tin man" whose exploits were summarized in the introduction.

2. Richard S. Tedlow, *The Watson Dynasty* (HarperBusiness, New York, 2003).

3. *Ibid.*, p. 103.

4. For Watson, it was a simple probability distribution. If "success" is randomly distributed or unpredictable, then the more you try the more likely you are to come good, despite inevitable failures along the way. Babe Ruth had a similar attitude. "Every strike," the legendary baseball player once said, "brings me closer to the next home run."

5. Quoted in Mark Pendergrast, *For God, Country and Coca-Cola: The Unauthorized History of the World's Most Popular Soft Drink* (Weidenfeld & Nicolson, London, 1993, p. 346).

6. It is estimated that if Steve Jobs loses his job over the share backdating controversy that rages as I write, Apple's share price will lose 20 percent of its current market value ($14 billion). *That's* how much one man matters!

7. See Pendergrast, *op. cit.*, especially pp. 210–11. The infamous New Coke episode is yet another example of denial marketing in action.

8. The more I think about this, the more I'm convinced that a kind of Customer Stockholm Syndrome is at work. The customer/victim transfers their allegiance to the marketer/captor who treats them abominably, then relents a little. It's well known in the customer-service literature that maltreated customers often turn into enthusiastic spokespersons for a brand after they've received minor reparation of some kind. Loyalty is engendered by adversity as well as abjection. Granted, the suffering of my readers hasn't done me much good in the undying loyalty stakes. But, hey, there's an exception to every rule. Right?

Also by Stephen Brown

"A marketing text written as a novel ... You cannot fail to be amused, entertained and engrossed by this gem of a book."
– *Marketer* magazine

"Pitch perfect."
– *Harvard Business Review*

ISBN 978–1-904879–88–6
£9.99; paperback

"Intelligent, well-informed, easy to read and relevant to the marketing community. Read this and some of its magic may rub off on you and your brand."
– *Brand Strategy* magazine

ISBN 978–1-904879–30–5
£7.99; paperback